Steck Vaughn

WONDERS OF SCIENCE

:ion

Matter, Motion, and Machines

Joan S. Gottlieb

C O N T E N T S

Return to Michelle Hunt
Room 3

**Meet your state standards with free blackline masters and links to other materials at
www.HarcourtAchieve.com/AchievementZone.
Click Steck-Vaughn Standards.**

Harcourt Achieve

Rigby • Steck-Vaughn

www.HarcourtAchieve.com
1.800.531.5015

Wonders of Science Program

❏ **The Earth and Beyond**

❏ **The Human Body**

❏ **Land Animals**

■ **Matter, Motion, and Machines**

❏ **Plant Life**

❏ **Water Life**

About the Author

Joan S. Gottlieb taught at the elementary and secondary levels
for more than ten years. She received a Ph.D. in education
from the University of South Carolina. Dr. Gottlieb holds B.A.,
B.S., and M.Ed. degrees from the University of Minnesota.

ISBN 0-7398-9185-5

1 2 3 4 5 6 7 8 862 11 10 09 08 07 06 05 04

Scope and Sequence

	UNIT 1	UNIT 2	UNIT 3	UNIT 4	UNIT 5	UNIT 6	UNIT 7	UNIT 8
The Human Body	How the Body Is Organized	Body Systems	More Body Systems	The Nervous System	Human Reproduction	Diseases	Avoiding Health Problems	First Aid
Land Animals	Animal Adaptations	Invertebrate Animals	Amphibians	Reptiles	Birds	Mammals	Conservation	
Plant Life	Plants Are Living Things	Flowers	Grasses and Cereals	Trees	Plants Used as Food	Plant Adaptations	Plant Products	Conservation
Water Life	Water Environments	Water Plants	Invertebrate Water Animals	Fish	Water Reptiles	Water Birds	Water Mammals	Conservation
The Earth and Beyond	The Solar System	Weather	Land and Water	Regions of Earth	Shaping the Surface	The Changing Earth	Materials of Earth	Conservation
Matter, Motion, and Machines	Matter *Communicating Classifying Observing*	Changes in Matter *Communicating Interpreting Data Inferring*	Nature's Energies *Communicating Classifying Making Models*	Sound and Light *Communicating Inferring Observing*	Magnetism and Electricity *Communicating Making Models Observing*	Motion and Forces *Communicating Making Models Inferring*	Machines *Communicating Classifying Interpreting Data*	Technology *Communicating Observing Inferring*

Wonders of Science Program

About the Program

Wonders of Science was developed for students with special needs, including students in special education programs, students receiving remedial instruction, and students in regular classes who read at a second-to-third-grade reading level. This six-book program presents current science topics in a simple, straightforward manner.

Wonders of Science was written by a classroom teacher who has faced the difficulties of teaching junior and senior high school special-needs students without suitable teaching materials. Like most teachers of special-needs classes, she invested uncountable hours preparing materials that would capture her students' interest and offer them a chance to succeed.

Wonders of Science is a result of field testing a variety of activities in classes with a wide range of reading abilities, intellectual capacities, ages, maturity levels, social backgrounds, interests, attention spans, and physical capabilities. The end result is a program designed to appeal to a wide variety of special-needs students. This program offers a structured curriculum, yet it helps students develop the much needed skill of working independently.

Features of the Program

❑ All lessons are complete on one or two pages. Brief reading selections provide students with successful experiences. Students with short attention spans are not frustrated by lesson length.

❑ Scientific vocabulary appears in boldfaced type. Each vocabulary word is also defined in the Glossary at the back of the book.

❑ In the Teacher's Edition, words that may be unfamiliar or difficult for students are underlined. These words may need further explanation.

❑ Assessment in the form of exercises is included in every lesson to check retention of important scientific concepts. Unit and Mastery Tests are also provided.

❑ A one-page review at the end of each unit helps prepare students for the unit test. Student performance on the review can be used to plan reteaching activities based on individual needs before students take the unit test.

❑ *Explore & Discover,* a self-directed, hands-on activity at the end of each unit, provides students with an opportunity to develop process skills and reinforce concepts taught in the unit. These activities call for easy-to-obtain and use materials. Students should be more comfortable with familiar materials than with expensive scientific hardware and apparatus. Yet the physical and cognitive skills used are the same.

❑ In each unit test, main ideas and scientific concepts are presented in a format that incorporates standardized test items as well as open-ended sections.

❑ Teaching Strategies for each lesson are provided in the Teacher's Edition. These strategies, in the form of activities, provide support, reinforcement, and extension of concepts through real-life application, hands-on activities, or discussion.

❑ A *Just for Fun* page for each unit is included in the Teacher's Edition. This blackline master presents key scientific concepts from the unit in a puzzle format and can be used as reinforcement.

❑ Special Projects in the Teacher's Edition are motivational activities that supplement and provide enrichment to each unit. Read through the projects before beginning a unit to determine when each is most helpful to your class.

❑ A two-part Mastery Test is included in the Teacher's Edition for assessing student comprehension of key concepts. The Mastery Test is written in the same format as the unit tests to ease test anxiety and promote student success.

Meet your state standards with free blackline masters and links to other materials at **www.HarcourtAchieve.com/AchievementZone**. Click **Steck-Vaughn Standards**.

Using the Program

The *Wonders of Science* program was designed to be used flexibly. You are encouraged to use the materials in a way that best meets the needs of your students. For example, you may wish to introduce the vocabulary words first, and then have students read each lesson independently. Or, for students who are able to work independently, you may encourage use of the Glossary as an aid for defining new scientific vocabulary.

All exercise directions are shown in color and are, therefore, easily distinguished. Each exercise format is repeated throughout the text so that students become familiar with the directions.

The design of each page is friendly and easy to use. All text is contained in a box to help students focus on the lesson. A color band runs down the side of the reading passage to cue the student on what to read. Directions are set in color to cue the student when a new activity starts. Photographs and art are used to reinforce and illustrate scientific concepts.

Correlation to
Benchmarks for Science Literacy

In an effort to guide reform in science, mathematics, and technology education, the American Association for the Advancement of Science published the report *Benchmarks for Science Literacy* in 1993. This report specifies how students should progress toward science literacy, recommending what they should know and be able to do by the time they reach certain grade levels. Intended as a tool for designing curriculum, *Benchmarks* describes levels of understanding and ability for *all* students. Steck-Vaughn's *Wonders of Science* provides special-needs students with opportunities to build the common core of learning recommended by *Benchmarks*. In *Matter, Motion, and Machines,* students can also explore their individual interests and abilities by examining topics such as lasers, superconductors, and nuclear energy.

Wonders of Science: Matter, Motion, and Machines will be useful in helping students attain the following specific science literacy goals set out in *Benchmarks*:

Chapter 1: THE NATURE OF SCIENCE
Section C: The Scientific Enterprise
Important contributions to the advancement of science, mathematics, and technology have been made by different kinds of people, in different cultures, at different times.

Section C: The Scientific Enterprise
No matter who does science and mathematics or invents things, or when or where they do it, the knowledge and technology that result can eventually become available to everyone in the world.

Chapter 3: THE NATURE OF TECHNOLOGY
Section A: Technology and Science
Technology is essential to science for such purposes as access to outer space and other remote locations, sample collection and treatment, measurement, data collection and storage, computation, and communication of information.

Section C: Issues in Technology
The human ability to shape the future comes from a capacity for generating knowledge and developing new technologies—and for communicating ideas to others.

Chapter 4: THE PHYSICAL SETTING
Section D: Structure of Matter
All matter is made up of atoms, which are far too small to see directly through a microscope. The atoms of any element are alike but are different from atoms of other elements. Atoms may stick together in well-defined molecules or may be packed together in large arrays. Different arrangements of atoms into groups compose all substances.

Section D: Structure of Matter
Atoms and molecules are perpetually in motion. Increased temperature means greater average energy of motion, so most substances expand when heated. In solids, the atoms are closely locked in position and can only vibrate. In liquids, the atoms or molecules have higher energy, are more loosely connected, and can slide past one another; some molecules may get enough energy to escape into a gas. In gases, the atoms or molecules have still more energy and are free of one another except during occasional collisions.

Section E: Energy Transformations
Energy cannot be created or destroyed, but only changed from one form into another.

Section E: Energy Transformations
Heat can be transferred through materials by the collisions of atoms or across space by radiation. If the material is fluid, currents will be set up in it that aid the transfer of heat.

Section F: Motion
Light from the sun is made up of a mixture of many different colors of light, even though to the eye the light looks almost white. Other things that give off or reflect light have a different mix of colors.

Section F: Motion
Something can be "seen" when light waves emitted or reflected by it enter the eye—just as something can be "heard" when sound waves from it enter the ear.

Section G: Forces of Nature
Electric currents and magnets can exert a force on each other.

Chapter 8: THE DESIGNED WORLD
Section C: Energy Sources and Use
Energy can change from one form to another, although in the process some energy is always converted to heat. Some systems transform energy with less loss of heat than others.

Section C: Energy Sources and Use
Different ways of obtaining, transforming, and distributing energy have different environmental consequences.

Section C: Energy Sources and Use
Electrical energy can be produced from a variety of energy sources and can be transformed into almost any other form of energy. Moreover, electricity is used to distribute energy quickly and conveniently to distant locations.

Section C: Energy Sources and Use
Energy from the sun (and the wind and water energy derived from it) is available indefinitely. Because the flow of energy is weak and variable, very large collection systems are needed. Other sources don't renew or renew only slowly.

Section E: Information Processing
An increasing number of people work at jobs that involve processing or distributing information. Because computers can do these tasks faster and more reliably, they have become standard tools both in the workplace and at home.

Chapter 10: HISTORICAL PERSPECTIVES
Section A: Displacing Earth from the Center of the Universe
The motion of an object is always judged with respect to some other object or point and so the idea of absolute motion or rest is misleading.

Chapter 12: HABITS OF MIND
Section D: Communication Skills
Organize information in simple tables and graphs and identify relationships they reveal.

Section D: Communication Skills
Read simple tables and graphs produced by others and describe in words what they show.

Master Materials List
Explore & Discover Activities

The following list is designed to help you acquire and keep track of materials for the **Explore & Discover** activities in this book. These materials are commonly available in classrooms, or may be purchased at supermarkets or discount stores, or brought from students' homes.

The quantities and groupings may be adjusted depending on the needs of your class, and in some cases you may want to substitute materials. The page numbers of the activities are provided to help your planning.

	Item	Quantity	Notes
Unit 1 **Matter** *page 18*	cups, clear plastic	1 per student	Also used in Units 2, 4
	water	enough to fill cups	
	food coloring, small bottles	4 or more per class	
	medicine droppers	4 or more per class	
Unit 2 **Changes in Matter** *page 34*	colored chalk	1 piece per student	
	scissors	1 pair per student	Also used in Unit 3
	bowls, small	1 per student	
	spoons, metal or wood	1 per student	
	water	1/4 cup per student	
	cups, plastic or paper (8 oz.)	1 per student	Also used in Units 1, 4
	filter paper or coffee filters	1 per student	
Unit 3 **Nature's Energies** *page 52*	spools, thread (empty)	1 per student	
	cartons, milk (any size)	1 per student	
	scissors	1 pair per student	Also used in Unit 2
	tape, masking or plastic	several rolls per class	Also used in Units 6, 7
	straws, drinking, or pencils	1 per student	Also used in Unit 6
	water, pitchers of	several per class	
	pans, large plastic	several per class	
Unit 4 **Sound and Light** *page 72*	cups, plastic or paper	1 per student	Also used in Units 1, 2
	plastic wrap	1 roll per class	
	rubber bands	1 per student	
	pepper	1 container per class	
	radio or tape player	1 per class	
	pans, metal baking	several per class	
	rulers	several per class	
Unit 5 **Magnetism and Electricity** *page 94*	cork, sliced, 1/8"–1/4" thick	1 slice per student	Prepare ahead of time.
	paper clips, small	1 per student	
	pans, plastic, rectangular	several per class	
	water	enough to fill pans	
	magnets, bar	several per class	
Unit 6 **Motion and Forces** *page 108*	string, length of classroom	1 piece per class	
	straws, drinking	1 per pair	Also used in Unit 3
	tape, masking	1 roll per class	Also used in Units 3, 7
	balloons	1 per pair	
Unit 7 **Machines** *page 124*	wood or heavy cardboard, 1' x 3'	1 per lab team	
	tape, masking	1 roll per lab team	Also used in Units 3, 6
	objects, small, flat (e.g., box of crayons)	1 per lab team	
	materials, smooth and rough	1 each per lab team	Suggestions on p. 124
	books	about 6 per lab team	
	watches with second hand	1 per lab team	
Unit 8 **Technology** *page 136*	paper, drawing	1 sheet per student	
	paper, lined, writing	1 sheet per student	

UNIT 1 Matter

The first two lessons of Unit 1 describe matter, including the distinction between mass and weight, and the four states of matter. The unit next discusses atoms and the three major subatomic particles and then moves on to elements. With this background the unit proceeds to metals and then metalloids, nonmetals, and inert gases, concluding with an explanation of the periodic table.

Page 4—What Is Matter?
Materials: construction paper, typing paper, small paper clip, thumbtack, two sizes of balls

Remind students that an object's weight is determined by the pull of gravity. Have students compare two objects that are about the same size, such as a paper clip and a thumbtack. Lead them in a discussion of how to discover which weighs more using gravity. Guide students to logically conclude that the more an object weighs the faster it will fall if dropped from the same height. Then have students experiment with gravity and weight using objects found in the classroom. Volunteers choose two objects that are about the same size, hold them up at the same level, and release them at the same time. The heavier object will fall to the ground first due to a stronger gravity pull.

Page 6—States of Matter
Materials: 1-foot-square piece of blotter paper, 50 checkers or buttons of the same size

Help students visualize how particles physically relate to each other in solids, liquids, and gases. Explain that each checker stands for a particle of matter. Have one student illustrate a solid by placing all the checkers on the blotter paper. The checkers should be lined up in columns and rows with all checkers touching other checkers. Have a second student illustrate a liquid. This student should use fewer checkers, and they should not be lined up regularly. Have a third student illustrate a gas. This student should use even fewer checkers, which should be far apart from each other.

Page 8—Atoms

Build on the concept that "different kinds of atoms are different from each other because they contain a different number of particles" by showing how the different kinds of atoms fall into a predictable pattern.

Draw the first five atoms of the periodic table on the chalkboard. (Draw a circle to represent the nucleus, and inside the circle write a number and *P* for protons and a number and *N* for neutrons; outside the circle, write a number and *E* for electrons.) After you draw the third atom, lithium, ask students about the fourth atom. How many protons does it have? How many neutrons? How many electrons? Students should find a pattern. (Each succeeding atom has one more proton, neutron, and electron than the one before.)

Page 10—Elements
Materials: small, heavyweight plastic bag; blue, red, and green marbles, about 10 of each

This activity may help students visualize how matter is composed of elements. Fill the bag with all the marbles. Tell students that the bag contains certain "matter" made of three kinds of elements represented by the three different colors. Have a student remove all the blue marbles. Ask the class how many different kinds of elements now make up the matter in the bag (two). Have another student remove all the red marbles. Ask how many kinds of elements there are now (one kind). Now ask if the "matter" can be broken down any further. (It cannot be. An element is the simplest form of matter.)

Page 12—Metals

Explain that *metal* has a specialized meaning for scientists. In common usage, steel is a metal. Steel is produced from the element iron mixed with other elements. To a scientist metals are elements. So steel is not a metal, but iron is. To a scientist not all metals are hard. For example, sodium is a metal that is not hard. Some metals that people need in their bodies to stay healthy are calcium, magnesium, copper, zinc, and iron.

Page 14—Metalloids, Nonmetals, and Inert Gases

Mnemonics may help students learn these categories. The suffix *-oid* means *similar to*. Students may have met this suffix in science fiction movies: *androids* are humanlike robots. *Non-* means *not*. Explain that inert gases are also called *noble gases.* Nobles did not readily mix with other people; similarly, noble gases do not readily mix with other elements.

Page 16—Periodic Table

Encourage students to speculate on how elements got their names and symbols. Explain that some symbols come from Latin names, such as Fe from *ferrum* (iron) and Cu from *cuprum* (copper). Ask students which country the names *americium* and *polonium,* for example, come from (America and Poland). Ask the following: Who were einsteinium and curium named after? (Einstein and Curie) Which planet names are found in *neptunium* and *plutonium?* (Neptune and Pluto) The imaginary planet that Superman came from was named after which element? (krypton)

Page 18—Investigate Particles in Liquids

Using the process skill *Observing,* students can see for themselves that particles diffuse, or spread out, in a liquid. Follow up by asking students what would happen if this activity was done with solids or with gases.

UNIT 2 Changes in Matter

In Unit 2, compounds, mixtures, and solutions are defined. Physical changes are distinguished from chemical changes. The explanation of chemical change leads to a lesson on chemical reactions, which focuses on how chemical reactions are written as chemical equations. Next, the three major types of compounds—acids, bases, and salts—are introduced, and some of their properties are described. The unit concludes with an overview of the presence of chemicals in everyday life.

Page 20—Molecules and Compounds

Write the formulas for several compounds—such as H_2O, CO_2, and NaCl—on the chalkboard. Explain that a subscript number after the symbol of an element indicates the number of atoms of that element in the molecule. If there is no subscript number, the number is understood to be 1. Rewrite each formula on the chalkboard as follows:

2 H + 1 O; 1 C + 2 O; 1 Na + 1 Cl.

Page 22—Mixtures

Materials: glass of water, spoon, salt

To a glass of water add one spoonful of salt and stir until it dissolves. Remind students that this kind of mixture—in which one substance dissolves in another—is a solution. Keep adding salt and stirring until no more salt dissolves in the water. Explain that a solution that will not dissolve any more of a solid is called a *saturated solution.*

Page 24—Physical Changes

Materials: sandpaper, small blocks of soft wood

Have students make a physical change. Distribute sandpaper and small pieces of wood to students and have them sand the wood. After they have gathered a small pile of sawdust, ask them to describe what has happened to the wood. (The shape of the wood has changed.) Be sure they understand that the sawdust is still wood, but it is wood in a different shape. A physical change has taken place.

Page 26—Chemical Changes

Begin a discussion of how the body gets the nutrients it needs from food. Ask what kind of change food undergoes as it is chewed. (Chewing is a physical change; solids are broken down into smaller pieces.) Explain that while food is being broken down this way, chemicals are released into the mouth. What kind of change is this? (a chemical change) The chemical composition of food changes as it goes through the process of digestion.

Page 28—Chemical Reactions

Emphasize that the right side of a chemical equation must show the exact same number of atoms as the left side. Make clear that it is the arrangement of atoms that changes in a chemical reaction; no atoms are ever lost. Illustrate with NaCl. On the chalkboard, write:

$Na + Cl_2 \longrightarrow NaCl$.

Explain that separate atoms of chlorine do not exist naturally, but 2 atoms combine as a molecule of chlorine (Cl_2). The left side of the equation has 1 sodium atom and 2 chlorine atoms, but the right side has one sodium atom and 1 chlorine atom. If 1 sodium atom is added to the left and 1 sodium and 1 chlorine atom are added to the right, both sides will have the exact same number of atoms. So the equation becomes:

$2Na + Cl_2 \longrightarrow 2NaCl$.

Page 30—Acids, Bases, and Salts

Common acids that students are probably familiar with are citric acid, which gives lemons and oranges their "bite"; carbonic acid, used to carbonate soft drinks; and boric acid, used as an eyewash. Point out that most soaps and detergents are bases. Explain that during digestion the stomach releases hydrochloric acid to break down food. When too much acid is released, a burning sensation can be experienced. Antacids are bases that combine with the excess acid and neutralize it.

Page 32—Chemicals Are Everywhere!

Materials: package labels, encyclopedia

Have students work in small groups and fill in charts that have the following headings: *Chemicals We Can Safely Eat; Harmful Chemicals in Food; Chemicals We Clean With; Household Chemicals That Can Be Dangerous.* As a part of their research, students can check package labels at home and in stores.

Page 34—Test for a Solution

This activity reinforces the process skill *Interpreting Data* as students test whether or not chalk and water make a solution. Note: If you use coffee filters, some of the chalk particles will go through. Students might want to filter the mixture a second time to see if additional chalk will be filtered out.

UNIT 3 Nature's Energies

Unit 3 opens with a definition of energy and four major types of energy: mechanical, heat, electric, and chemical. The lesson on solar energy explains that all energy comes from the sun, preparing students for the lessons on heat, wind, water, steam, and nuclear energy. The unit ends with a look at present energy use and future energy needs.

Page 36—What Is Energy?

Materials: poster board, drawing paper, magazines, scissors, glue, marking pens

Begin a discussion on the various uses of mechanical, heat, electric, and chemical energy in everyday life. Then have students make posters about each type of energy. The posters may have originally drawn pictures or illustrations from magazines with appropriate captions. For example, a picture of a girl walking might be captioned, *She uses mechanical energy to walk to school.*

Page 38—Energy from the Sun

Make sure students understand that there would be no life on Earth if there were no sun. Ask them to name some benefits of solar energy. (The sun gives light and heat.) Tell students that solar energy also makes water evaporate. This water returns to Earth as rain and snow, keeping Earth's water supply replenished. Plants change solar energy into chemical energy when they make their own food.

Page 40—Heat Energy

Help students remember the distinction between convection and radiation by discussing the cooking of a hot dog. Convection makes it possible to cook a hot dog over a campfire. The air around the fire is heated and rises in currents. The hot air currents cook the hot dog. Radiation cooks a hot dog beneath an electric broiler or a microwave oven. The broiler's hot wires give off infrared rays of light and heat that travel down into the hot dog. In a microwave oven, tiny sound waves penetrate the inside of the hot dog producing heat energy.

Page 42—Wind Energy

Explain why there is often a cool breeze near the sea. As hot air rises, cooler air moves into the area left by the hot air. Air over the ocean is cooler than air over land. Warm air over the land rises, and the cool ocean air moves into the space.

Page 44—Water Energy

Lead a discussion in which students contribute experiences or information about the power of water. For example, they may cite the force of water from a hose, or the experience of being pushed by waves in the ocean. Some students may mention how rain can wash away soil.

Page 46—Steam Energy

Remind students that in a liquid like water, the molecules move around to fit whatever container they are in. But as molecules absorb heat energy, the water is changed to steam. The water molecules in steam move around at a much greater speed, colliding frequently and rebounding farther after collisions. The space between molecules increases. Thus the steam expands enormously. If the steam is contained, it presses with great force against the walls of its container. This powerful force can move the heavy wheels of a turbine.

Page 48—Nuclear Energy

Clarify for students two different uses of the word *radiation*. In one sense radiation is a form of heat transfer. Radiation also refers to the energy emitted in the form of particles or waves when atomic nuclei are split. This radiation is mostly gamma rays. Gamma rays easily pass through the body, injuring cells and leading to cancer. The danger of leaks of gamma radiation is one reason people oppose nuclear energy.

Page 50—Our Energy Needs

Have students describe ways they know that people use such energy sources as electricity, gasoline, oil, and coal. Ask students which energy sources lead to pollution. They should be familiar with the pollution from exhausts of cars and buses that burn gasoline. They may also cite factory smokestacks that pollute the air. Remind them that nuclear reactors produce radioactive wastes.

Page 52—Make a Water Wheel

Students use the process skill *Making Models* as they investigate how a water wheel—and a windmill—

works. As a follow-up to the activity, you might like to provide library books with illustrations of old water wheels, modern water turbines, and historic and contemporary windmills.

UNIT 4 Sound and Light

In Unit 4 sound is explained as energy that moves through matter as a wave, causing the matter's molecules to vibrate. Next, pitch and loudness are discussed, and then music is distinguished from noise. The section on sound ends with the anatomy of hearing and talking. The second part of the unit opens with an explanation of how light travels, going on to establish sources of light. The next two lessons take up color and lenses. The unit ends by describing the anatomy of sight.

Page 54—How Sound Travels
Materials: basin, water

Pour some water into a basin. When the water is still, let a drop of water fall onto the surface. Circular waves will form. Explain that sound moves away from its source in waves, the way water waves move away from where the drop hit the surface. Then draw a regularly wavy line on the chalkboard, explaining that it is how a wave looks from the side. Have students identify and label the crest, trough, amplitude, and wavelength.

Page 56—Pitch and Loudness

Remind students that sound is produced by the movement of molecules in matter. The speed, or frequency, of the sound waves depends on the type of matter that the sound waves travel through. Ask students which type of matter—solid, liquid, or gas—sound waves move fastest through. (Sound waves move more quickly through dense matter, or solids.) Which kind of matter do sound waves travel the slowest through? (gas)

Page 58—Music
Materials: poster board, magazines, marking pens, scissors, glue

Have students work in small groups to make music posters. Have students glue on the poster board magazine illustrations of their favorite musicians playing instruments. Students should label each illustration with a statement describing the instrument's sound and explaining which part of the instrument vibrates to make that sound.

Page 60—How You Hear

Review for students the path taken by sound waves, and have students tell which kind of matter is involved at each step. The outside ear is a solid. It catches sound waves that move down the auditory canal, which is filled with air, a gas. The sound waves make the eardrum, a solid, vibrate, and the vibrations are passed on to the inner ear, which is filled with a liquid. The moving liquid bends hairs, solids, felt by the auditory nerves that lead to the brain, both solids.

Page 62—How You Talk

Amplify this lesson by explaining that the larynx and vocal cords produce sound in much the same way as a stringed instrument does. The larynx is like the body of the instrument, and the vocal cords are like the strings. On an instrument like the violin, the strings that produce low sounds are thicker and looser than the strings that produce high sounds. When you talk the vocal cords become tighter or looser, producing higher- or lower-pitched sounds.

Page 64—How Light Travels
Materials: teacup or shallow bowl, water, coin

Demonstrate to students that light waves are affected by the type of matter they pass through. Put a teacup on a table and place a coin in the center. Have each student, one at a time, stand by the table so that he or she views the inside of the cup at a 45° angle and cannot see the coin. Gently pour water into the cup, without disturbing the coin. The coin will become visible to the student. Explain that light was "bent" by the water, bringing the coin into the line of vision.

Page 66—Sources of Light

Ask why it is difficult to see objects at night or in a dark room. (There is no light.) Light from some source—the sun or a light bulb—must hit an object and be reflected in order for the object to be visible. Light-colored objects reflect more light than objects with dark colors. Have students compare pairs of objects in the classroom, stating which reflects more light.

Page 67—Color

Ask students why the sky is blue. Explain that the spectrum is made up of seven colors: red, orange, yellow, green, blue, indigo, and violet. Light from the sun contains all seven colors. Each color has a different wavelength, and each wavelength is affected differently as it passes through different matter. During the day, the sky is blue because some of the blue light is reflected, or separated out from the spectrum, by particles of dust and other matter in the air.

Page 68—Lenses

Materials: newspaper, wax paper, glycerine

Help students understand how the refraction of light by a convex lens magnifies an image. Place wax paper over a newspaper. Put a drop of glycerine on the wax paper. The text below the glycerine will be enlarged by the refraction of light through the convex drop.

Page 70—How You See

Tell students that the retina has structures called *cones* that allow the perception of color. People with normal vision see all colors. But some people perceive only yellow and blue, the other colors are perceived as tones of gray. Other people see only tones of gray.

Page 72—Make Pepper Jump

With this two-part activity, students use the process skill *Observing* to see a sound wave hit an object and make it vibrate, too.

Mastery Test, Part A, covering units 1–4 can be found on page T15.

UNIT 5   Magnetism and Electricity

Unit 5 begins with electricity, describing it in terms of the behavior of electric charges. Next, the unit treats electric currents, circuits, and other applications of electricity. Magnetism is introduced, and its relation to electricity is explained. The unit ends with lessons on electric motors, electronics, and the safe use of electricity.

Page 74—What Is Electricity?

Materials: two balloons, two 1-foot lengths of string, nylon cloth

Demonstrate how charges attract and repel. Blow up each balloon and tie its end. Attach one string to each balloon. Then tie the loose ends of the two strings together. Rub each balloon with cloth. Suspend the two balloons in the air by holding the string. The balloons will swing away from each other. Ask students to explain this. (Rubbing the balloons gave each of them a positive electric charge; like charges—in this case, two positive charges—repel.) Put your hand between the two balloons. Both balloons will be attracted to it. Ask students to explain. (The balloons and your hand have opposite charges; opposite charges attract.)

Page 76—Electric Currents

Review with students some materials that are good conductors (metals, along with acids, bases, and salts when they are dissolved in water) and those that are good insulators (wood, glass, rubber, dry air). Have students describe insulators they are familiar with (insulated electric wires and handles of metal cooking utensils). Ask why conductors should be insulated. (Heat and electricity will not be transferred to people or objects nearby.)

Page 78—Electric Circuits and Volts

Clarify the relationship between electricity and heat. Ask students if they have ever noticed the plug of an appliance, such as an air conditioner, becoming warm. Explain that even though conductors allow an electron flow, they still resist it. This resistance generates heat. The greater the electric current that flows through a wire, the greater the heat generated. Large appliances, such as air conditioners and refrigerators, use more current than small appliances, such as lamps and irons.

Page 80—Fuses and Circuit Breakers

Materials: household fuse

Pass around a fuse to students. Explain that when electricians wire a house, they install only as many electric outlets as the wiring system can handle. A common cause of burned-out fuses is overloading. People may put a multiple-outlet plug in an outlet designed for only one plug. When several appliances are plugged in and drawing electricity, the overloading blows out a fuse. Ask students if they have ever had a fuse "blow" in their home.

Page 82—Dry Cells and Batteries

Begin a discussion of everyday uses of dry cells and batteries by asking students to name items they are familiar with that use them (flashlights, hand-held calculators, some types of cameras, portable radios, automobiles).

Page 84—What Is Magnetism?

Materials: bar magnet, steel wool, scissors, cardboard

Show students that a magnetic field has lines of force that form certain patterns. Cut the steel wool into tiny filings and spread them out on the cardboard. Put the board on a bar magnet and tap the board gently a few times. The filings will line up in the curved patterns of a magnetic field.

Page 86—Electromagnets

Materials: flashlight dry cell; 10-foot length of thin, insulated wire; 2-inch iron nail; small iron washers or tacks; pliers

Help students make an electromagnet. Have a student wind as much wire as possible around a nail, leaving one foot of wire free at both ends. Have another student remove some insulation from both free ends of the wire. Another student should touch the ends of the wires to dry cell terminals. Test this electromagnet by picking up small iron objects with one end of the nail. Ask students to predict what will happen to the objects held by the nail when the wires do not touch the terminals. (The current stops, and any objects held by the nail fall off.)

Page 88—Electric Motors and Generators

Amplify the basic principle of an electric motor. An alternating electric current is passed through a stationary electromagnet, making the poles of the magnet change with each reversal of the current. Close to the stationary electromagnet is a second electromagnet, which is free to rotate. This electromagnet is alternately attracted and repelled by the stationary magnet, causing it to rotate continually on its axis and to produce mechanical energy.

Page 90—Electronics

Explain that electronic devices control the movement of electrons more carefully than alternating current. Remind students that electrons moving in a current generate considerable heat. Semiconductors, which are electronic devices, generate much less heat. Electronic devices also need smaller amounts of conductive materials and require less current. Transistors, for example, can magnify electric current.

Page 92—Using Electricity Safely

Materials: poster board, marking pens

Have students work in small groups to make posters illustrating safety precautions with electric appliances. Students may illustrate a potential hazard, such as using wet hands to turn on an appliance, and add a caution, *Keep Electrons Dry!*

Page 94—Make a Magnetic Racer

In this activity students will practice the process skill *Observing*. In order to be successful competitors, students will need to notice through trial and error the optimum distance between their magnet and their racer.

UNIT 6 Motion and Forces

Unit 6 opens with a discussion of a frame of reference in which the sensation of motion is shown to be a relative phenomenon. The next lesson defines speed, velocity, and acceleration. Balanced and unbalanced forces and gravity are then discussed, followed by the laws of motion. The unit concludes with a discussion of how knowledge of motion and force make space travel possible.

Page 96—What Is Motion?

Explain that anything at all can be used as a frame of reference. What is the frame of reference for someone watching a bird moving across an empty sky? (the position of the person's body) For motion on the surface of Earth, the most convenient frame of reference is often Earth itself. The motion of the planets, however, is much easier to explain if the sun is used as the frame of reference.

Page 98—Speed, Velocity, and Acceleration

Materials: book, wooden ruler with a groove in it, marble, stopwatch

Demonstrate speed, velocity, and acceleration. Place a book on the floor and make a ramp with a ruler. Measure a distance of six feet from the top of the ruler to some point on the floor. Roll a marble in the groove down the ruler, noting on the stopwatch the time the marble takes to travel the six feet. Repeat the activity several times. Calculate speed by dividing the distance (six feet) by the time. Ask students if the marble's velocity changed. (Yes, when the marble reached the floor, its speed probably changed and its direction definitely changed.) Ask students if the marble accelerated as it traveled down the ramp. (Yes, a change in velocity is acceleration.)

Page 100—Balanced and Unbalanced Forces

Have students analyze common everyday movements they make in terms of push-pull forces. For example, walking is initiated by pushing the back foot against the ground; writing involves pushing a pen across a page; lifting an object is a pull force.

Page 102—Gravity

Explain that even stationary objects have a force acting on them, and this force is gravity. Gravity is a pull force. A book lying on a table is actually being pulled against the table. Ask students why a book on a table is not pulled through the table. (The table exerts an upward force against the book that is greater than the downward pull of gravity.)

Page 104—Laws of Motion

Give students an example of Newton's first law of motion which states that an object at rest will remain at rest until the forces become unbalanced by some other force. Ask students to imagine a game of tug-of-war. Ask what will happen if team A and team B both pull with the same amount of force. (Nothing happens. The forces are balanced.) Then ask what will happen if team A pulls with more force than team B. (The forces will become unbalanced. Team B will be pulled toward team A—that is, in the direction of the larger force.)

Page 106—Space Travel

Explain why a satellite moving in space is not pulled back to Earth by the force of Earth's gravity. Remind students of Newton's first law of motion: An object in motion will remain in motion as long as the forces acting on it are balanced. The satellite's motion—a speed of five miles per second—is balanced by the force of gravity. If the satellite's speed were slower, the force of gravity would be stronger, pulling the satellite to Earth. Also, if the satellite's speed were greater, the force of gravity would not be strong enough to keep the satellite from flying off into outer space.

Page 108—Make a Balloon Rocket

Students use the process skill *Making Models* to see how the law of action-reaction works. Give other examples and ask students to explain the forces. (For example, jumping from boat to dock: you push on boat; boat pushes on you.)

UNIT 7 Machines

Unit 7 opens with a scientific definition of *work*. The next lesson describes friction as a force. With this background, students are prepared for lessons on machines in general, simple machines, and compound machines. The unit concludes with lessons on gasoline engines and jet engines.

Page 110—What Is Work?

In the scientific sense, *work* is using force to move an object. Both the force used and the motion must be in the same direction. Therefore, pushing an object away or lifting an object is work because the object moves in the direction of the force. If the object does not move, no work has happened.

Page 112—Friction

Materials: various classroom objects, sandpaper

Have students demonstrate that rough surfaces provide more friction than smooth surfaces. Have students slide various objects, one by one, along a piece of sandpaper on a table and along the table without the sandpaper. There is less friction with the smoother surface (without the sandpaper).

Page 114—What Are Machines?

Materials: large, full, round can

Machines with wheels make work easier because wheels lessen friction. Have students place a can upright on the floor and push it. Then, have them put the can on its side and push it so it rolls. Ask if more or less force was needed the second time (less). Explain that when the can is upright, the whole surface of the bottom of the can rubs against the floor. When the can is on its side, only a small area touches the floor at any one time, thus generating less friction between the two surfaces.

Page 116—Simple Machines

On the chalkboard, write the six simple machines as headings for six columns. Ask students to write everyday simple machines they know under the appropriate headings. For example, baseball bats under *Levers,* ramps under *Inclined Planes,* knife blades under *Wedges,* bottle caps under *Screws,* string-drawn blinds under *Pulleys,* and doorknobs under *Wheels and Axles.*

Page 118—Compound Machines

Have students work in pairs to make a list of seven compound machines with which they are familiar.

Students should identify the simple machines that form the compound machines.

Page 120—Gasoline Engines

Tell students that although gasoline is used in engines in liquid form, it is the energy that it gives off as a gas that makes it a useful fuel. When the spark plugs ignite the gasoline, it turns from a liquid into a gas. Remind students that gases expand with great force. It is the force of this expanding gas that induces the mechanical energy of the pistons, crankshaft, and wheels.

Page 122—Jet Engines

Tell students that car and jet engines are examples of internal combustion engines, or engines that burn fuel inside the engine. (The steam engine and the turbine are external combustion engines.) The fuel used in internal combustion engines mixes with air. Air is a flammable gas and helps fuel to burn. Students who have built campfires or have started a fire in a fireplace should be familiar with the flammability of air. A small flame is usually generated, and then it is blown on, to mix air with the burning wood.

Page 124—Find Out About Friction

Students will collect and graph data, then use the process skill *Interpreting Data* to explain what happened during their investigation. For more accurate results, students might time the slide on each material twice and record the average time.

UNIT 8   Technology

Computers, lasers, and robots are discussed in the first three lessons of Unit 8. The word *technology* is defined, and some modern methods of communication are described. The unit ends with an introduction to the technology of the future.

Page 126—Computers

Have students work in small groups and compose a list of places where computers are used, indicating also how they are used. For example, students might list their school as a place where computers are found, and they might note that one function of the computer is to produce the school newspaper.

Page 128—Lasers

Students may be familiar with holograms, the three-dimensional images created by lasers. Holographic images appear on some toys and book covers. They can be used in place of projected photographic images. In medical schools, holographic projections may be used to show realistic images of surgical procedures.

Page 130—Robots

Invite students to name types of jobs robots can do. Have students discuss whether it is better for a robot or a human to do each type of job and give reasons why. If necessary, tell students that robots cannot think on their own. Robots must be programmed to perform certain tasks. Robots perform many tasks that are very dangerous to people. Robots perform tasks that require a great deal of precision and robots do not grow tired, as people do.

Page 132—Communications

Discuss with students the ways their lives are affected by modern communications. Have them list information they get through these new technologies (for example, they can get news "live" from other parts of the world). Discuss how the world is "getting smaller" now that people can communicate easily over long distances. Ask students how this can affect relations between countries.

Page 134—Technology of the Future

Materials: computer and technology magazines, poster board, markers, scissors, glue

Have students research new forms of technology and machines they would like to use. Ask them to cut out or draw an example of their findings. Then have them write a paragraph about how they would utilize the technology or machine in their daily life.

Page 136—Design a Robot

Based on their knowledge of tasks that are performed by robots, students will use the process skill *Inferring* to design a robot to perform a school or household task or to do work in the community.

Mastery Test, Part B, covering units 5–8 can be found on page T17.

Mastery Test

Fill in the circle in front of the word or phrase that best completes each sentence. The first one is done for you.

1. Anything that takes up space and has mass is
   - ⓐ a solid.
   - ● matter.
   - ⓒ an element.

2. The pull of gravity upon a body or an object is called
   - ⓐ matter.
   - ⓑ mass.
   - ⓒ weight.

3. The particles in atoms have different
   - ⓐ electric charges.
   - ⓑ gases.
   - ⓒ flavors.

4. A molecule is a group of
   - ⓐ atoms.
   - ⓑ elements.
   - ⓒ mixtures.

5. Every molecule in a compound is
   - ⓐ different.
   - ⓑ soft.
   - ⓒ exactly the same.

6. All the energy in the world comes from
   - ⓐ machines.
   - ⓑ wind.
   - ⓒ the sun.

7. Sound waves with a high frequency have a
   - ⓐ loud sound.
   - ⓑ low sound.
   - ⓒ high sound.

8. When light rays hit a smooth, shiny surface and bounce back, it is called
   - ⓐ reflection.
   - ⓑ concave.
   - ⓒ amplitude.

9. Chemical changes always make
   - ⓐ water.
   - ⓑ new substances.
   - ⓒ acids.

10. Energy is the ability to
    - ⓐ do work.
    - ⓑ smell.
    - ⓒ see.

Mastery Test

Use the words below to complete the sentences.

| compounds | liquid | refraction |
| elements | radiation | |

11. Molecules of more than one element can make _____.

12. A solid or a gas can become a _____.

13. Matter in its simplest form consists of _____.

14. When an atom splits, it gives off _____.

15. The bending of light rays by things in their path is called

_____.

Fill in the missing words.

16. A _____ change is any change in matter that does not change the matter's molecules. (physical, chemical)

17. Heat energy passes through solids by _____. (convection, conduction)

18. Because Earth _____ you see the sun's light only during the day. (reflects, rotates)

19. Light is given off in tiny particles called _____. (electrons, photons)

Write the answer on the lines.

20. What are the three kinds of particles found in an atom?

_____

_____

_____

Mastery Test

Fill in the circle in front of the word or phrase that best completes each sentence. The first one is done for you.

1. The attracting area around every magnet is
   - ⓐ electricity.
   - ● a magnetic field.
   - ⓒ a terminal.

2. Any push or pull is
   - ⓐ speed.
   - ⓑ gravity.
   - ⓒ a force.

3. If a force is used on an object and the object moves in the same direction as the force, it is
   - ⓐ a machine.
   - ⓑ an engine.
   - ⓒ work.

4. Motion depends on
   - ⓐ a frame of reference.
   - ⓑ speed.
   - ⓒ time.

5. An object at rest
   - ⓐ will stay at rest.
   - ⓑ will start moving.
   - ⓒ is unbalanced.

6. Electric motors change electric energy into
   - ⓐ mechanical energy.
   - ⓑ magnetism.
   - ⓒ chemical energy.

7. A machine cannot make
   - ⓐ energy.
   - ⓑ friction.
   - ⓒ heat.

8. If machines can be made that understand speech, then we will have
   - ⓐ artificial intelligence.
   - ⓑ computers.
   - ⓒ lasers.

9. Work is made easier by
   - ⓐ forces.
   - ⓑ motions.
   - ⓒ machines.

10. The spot where a laser hits becomes
    - ⓐ cold.
    - ⓑ diseased.
    - ⓒ hot.

Mastery Test

Fill in the missing words.

11. Things that have _____ electric charges attract each other. (the same, opposite)

12. The more mass matter has the _____ the force of its gravity. (less, greater)

13. Speed in a certain direction is _____. (velocity, acceleration)

14. The attraction we can see between two objects with opposite electric charges is called _____ electricity. (static, current)

Write the word or words that best finish each sentence.

15. _____ are metals that attract and repel other pieces of metal.

16. _____ are machines that can store and work with information.

17. Friction is a force that _____, or works against, motion.

18. A _____ is an object that orbits, or moves around, Earth.

19. _____ light is much stronger than natural light.

Write the answer on the lines.

20. What is one way that machines make work easier?

_____

_____

_____

Mastery Test

Fill in the circle in front of the word or phrase that best completes each sentence. The first one is done for you.

1. Anything that takes up space and has mass is
   - (a) a solid.
   - ● matter.
   - (c) an element.

2. The pull of gravity upon a body or an object is called
   - (a) matter.
   - (b) mass.
   - (c) weight.

3. The particles in atoms have different
   - (a) electric charges.
   - (b) gases.
   - (c) flavors.

4. A molecule is a group of
   - (a) atoms.
   - (b) elements.
   - (c) mixtures.

5. Every molecule in a compound is
   - (a) different.
   - (b) soft.
   - (c) exactly the same.

6. All the energy in the world comes from
   - (a) machines.
   - (b) wind.
   - (c) the sun.

7. Sound waves with a high frequency have a
   - (a) loud sound.
   - (b) low sound.
   - (c) high sound.

8. When light rays hit a smooth, shiny surface and bounce back, it is called
   - (a) reflection.
   - (b) concave.
   - (c) amplitude.

9. Chemical changes always make
   - (a) water.
   - (b) new substances.
   - (c) acids.

10. Energy is the ability to
    - (a) do work.
    - (b) smell.
    - (c) see.

T15

Mastery Test

Use the words below to complete the sentences.

compounds	liquid	refraction
elements	radiation	

11. Molecules of more than one element can make _____ compounds _____.
12. A solid or a gas can become a _____ liquid _____.
13. Matter in its simplest form consists of _____ elements _____.
14. When an atom splits, it gives off _____ radiation _____.
15. The bending of light rays by things in their path is called _____ refraction _____.

Fill in the missing words.

16. A _____ physical _____ change is any change in matter that does not change the matter's molecules. (physical, chemical)
17. Heat energy passes through solids by _____ conduction _____. (convection, conduction)
18. Because Earth _____ rotates _____ you see the sun's light only during the day. (reflects, rotates)
19. Light is given off in tiny particles called _____ photons _____. (electrons, photons)

Write the answer on the lines.

20. What are the three kinds of particles found in an atom?
    _____ Atoms are made up of positively charged protons, _____
    _____ negatively charged electrons, and neutral neutrons. _____

T16

Mastery Test

Fill in the circle in front of the word or phrase that best completes each sentence. The first one is done for you.

1. The attracting area around every magnet is
   - (a) electricity.
   - ● a magnetic field.
   - (c) a terminal.

2. Any push or pull is
   - (a) speed.
   - (b) gravity.
   - (c) a force.

3. If a force is used on an object and the object moves in the same direction as the force, it is
   - (a) a machine.
   - (b) an engine.
   - (c) work.

4. Motion depends on
   - (a) a frame of reference.
   - (b) speed.
   - (c) time.

5. An object at rest
   - (a) will stay at rest.
   - (b) will start moving.
   - (c) is unbalanced.

6. Electric motors change electric energy into
   - (a) mechanical energy.
   - (b) magnetism.
   - (c) chemical energy.

7. A machine cannot make
   - (a) energy.
   - (b) friction.
   - (c) heat.

8. If machines can be made that understand speech, then we will have
   - (a) artificial intelligence.
   - (b) computers.
   - (c) lasers.

9. Work is made easier by
   - (a) forces.
   - (b) motions.
   - (c) machines.

10. The spot where a laser hits becomes
    - (a) cold.
    - (b) diseased.
    - (c) hot.

T17

Mastery Test

Fill in the missing words.

11. Things that have _____ opposite _____ electric charges attract each other. (the same, opposite)
12. The more mass matter has the _____ greater _____ the force of its gravity. (less, greater)
13. Speed in a certain direction is _____ velocity _____. (velocity, acceleration)
14. The attraction we can see between two objects with opposite electric charges is called _____ static _____ electricity. (static, current)

Write the word or words that best finish each sentence.

15. _____ Magnets _____ are metals that attract and repel other pieces of metal.
16. _____ Computers _____ are machines that can store and work with information.
17. Friction is a force that _____ resists _____, or works against, motion.
18. A _____ satellite _____ is an object that orbits, or moves around, Earth.
19. _____ Laser _____ light is much stronger than natural light.

Write the answer on the lines.

20. What is one way that machines make work easier?
    _____ Answers may vary but should include: some machines cut down on _____
    _____ friction, some machines can change the amount of force used, _____
    _____ or some machines can change the direction of the force used. _____

T18

T19

Just for Fun

Fill in the missing words in each sentence. Use the words below.

atomic	gravity	mass	table
charges	leaf	metals	weight
element	liquid	solid	

1. Elements that are shiny and conduct heat are _ _ _ _ _ _ .
   14   7

2. How much matter an object has is its _ _ _ _ .
   10

3. The number of protons in the nucleus of an atom of an element is its
   _ _ _ _ _ _ number.
   18   5 17

4. The force that pulls matter toward the ground is _ _ _ _ _ _ _ .
   6   20

5. The simplest form of matter is an _ _ _ _ _ _ _ .
   21   11

6. The pull of gravity on an object is the object's _ _ _ _ _ _ .
   4   19

7. Elements are organized in a periodic _ _ _ _ _ .
   1 12   3

8. Electrons have negative _ _ _ _ _ _ _ .
   2   22

9. A brick is a _ _ _ _ _ .
   15   8

10. The metal gold can be made into sheets of gold _ _ _ _ .
    16

11. Milk is a _ _ _ _ _ _ .
    9   13

Solve the Secret Message. When a letter of a word above has a number under it, write that letter above the same number in the Secret Message.

Secret Message:

_ _ _   _ _ _ _ _   _ _   _ _ _ _ _   _ _   _ _ _ _ _ _ .
1 2 3   4 5 6 7 8   9 10   11 12 13 14   15 16   17 18 19 20 21 22

Just for Fun

Use the clues to complete the puzzle. Choose from the words below.

acids	chemical	liquid	salt
ashes	energy	medicine	solution
bases	heat	rust	water

Across

3. When wood burns, it turns into smoke and this.
6. Lemonade is an example of this kind of mixture.
8. H_2O is the formula for this.
10. This helps your body fight disease.
11. A solid and a gas can both become this.

Down

1. These are compounds that feel soapy and slippery and have molecules with a negative electric charge.
2. Baking causes this kind of change.
4. Iron atoms join with oxygen atoms to form molecules of this new substance.
5. In a chemical change, this causes the atoms to break free of their molecules and form different molecules.
7. This can make water evaporate to become steam.
9. These are compounds that taste sour and have molecules with a positive electric charge.

Just for Fun

Each sentence below is about a source of energy. But one word in each sentence is scrambled. Unscramble the letters. Then write the correct word on the lines at the right. Choose from the words below. The first one is done for you.

atom	gasoline	oil	steam
electric	live	radiation	water
energy	nuclear	rivers	years

1. METSA is made in a boiler.   **S T E A M**

2. Someday the supply of coal, LIO, and gasoline will run out.   _ _ _

3. Nothing on Earth could IVLE without the sun.   _ _ _ _

4. When the nucleus of an MOTA splits, it gives off a very large amount of energy.   _ _ _ _

5. Dams are built on SERVIR and lakes.   _ _ _ _ _ _

6. Many large CRILETEC power plants have steam turbines.   _ _ _ _ _ _ _ _

7. Many people think that RENCULA energy is too dangerous to use.   _ _ _ _ _ _ _

8. There are several kinds of YENGER.   _ _ _ _ _ _

9. Heat from the sun comes to you in TORADINIA waves.   _ _ _ _ _ _ _ _ _

10. NIGOLASE has chemical energy stored in it.   _ _ _ _ _ _ _ _

11. Coal and oil were formed from plants and animals millions of RESAY ago.   _ _ _ _ _

Solve the Secret Message. Find the first letters of all the words that you unscrambled and write them in order on the lines below.

Secret Message: The most important kind of energy is

_ _ _ _ _   _ _ _ _ _ _ .
1 2 3 4 5   6 7 8 9 10 11

Just for Fun

Choose from the words below to answer the questions.

bend	energy	music	vocal
crest	iris	pitch	waves
eardrum	lenses	trough	

1. What part of your ear vibrates?

    _ _ _ _ _ _ _
                     8

2. What kind of sound is made of notes?

    _ _ _ _ _
        3

3. What is the lowest part of a wave?

    _ _ _ _ _ _
    13   2

4. What is the colored part of your eye?

    _ _ _ _
    10   1

5. What is based on the frequency of a sound's waves?

    _ _ _ _ _
            12

6. How do sound and light move?

    _ _ _ _ _
      6

7. What do lenses do to light rays?

    _ _ _ _
      4 5

8. What cords vibrate when you talk?

    _ _ _ _ _
           9

9. What are used in microscopes?

    _ _ _ _ _ _
        7

10. What is light, music or energy?

    _ _ _ _ _ _
          11

Now find the letters that have numbers below them. Write those letters below. When you are finished, you will have the answer to a riddle.

Riddle: What kinds of energy move in waves?

_ _ _ _ _   _ _ _   _ _ _ _ _
1 2 3 4 5   6 7 8   9 10 11 12 13

UNIT 5

Just for Fun

Use the clues to solve the puzzle. Use the words below.

another	electricity	lift	rid
atom	good	magnetism	safely
charged	iron	one	terminals
compasses			

Across

1. The north pole of one magnet attracts the south pole of _____ magnet.

4. An electromagnet can _____ tons of iron.

6. When electrons leave their atoms, matter becomes electrically _____.

7. The force that magnets have is _____.

9. As long as an _____ has the same number of protons and electrons, the atom has no charge.

10. An electromagnet has an _____ bar inside a coil of wire.

12. It is important to use electricity _____.

Down

2. The electric outlets in your house provide alternating current _____.

3. An atom that loses, or gets _____ of electrons, has a positive charge.

5. A dry cell has two posts called _____.

6. Sailors use _____ to tell which direction they are going.

8. Rubber is a _____ insulator.

11. A magnet has a north pole at _____ end and a south pole at the other end.

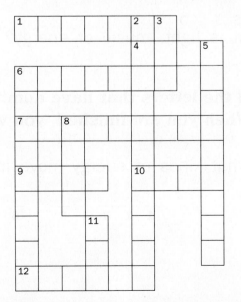

Just for Fun

UNIT 6

Each sentence below is about motion and forces. But one word in each sentence is scrambled. Unscramble the letters. Then write the correct word on the spaces at the right. Choose from the words below. The first one is done for you.

differ	lift	speeds
force	motion	time
gravity	never	velocity

1. Any push or pull is a COFER.

<u>F</u> <u>O</u> <u>R</u> <u>C</u> <u>E</u>
1   15

2. YETCOVIL is speed in a certain direction.

— — — — — — — —
         9   6

3. Speed is the distance something moves in a certain MITE.

— — — —
    4 11

4. Forces FIDREF in size and direction.

— — — — — —
      10 13 2

5. Powerful engines are needed to FLIT rockets into space.

— — — —
   7

6. VAYTRIG attracts matter.

— — — — — — —
  8 3

7. An object at rest will VEREN move if balanced forces act on it.

— — — — —
14   12

8. It is positive acceleration if a car DESEPS up.

— — — — — —
   16 5

Solve the Secret Message. When a letter of a word above has a number under it, write that letter above the same number in the Secret Message.

Secret Message: To tell if something is in motion, you need a

— — — — —   — —   — — — — — — — — —.
1 2 3 4 5   6 7   8 9 10 11 12 13 14 15 16

Just for Fun

The following sentences are about machines. But one word is missing in each sentence. Write in the missing words on the spaces at the right. Choose from the words below. The first letter of each missing word is written in for you. Read the letters down the first column for a message about machines.

axle	energy	move	resists
car	heat	needs	simple
complex	inclined	out	wedge
down	kind	own	

1. To do work, a force must _____ something. M _ _ _

2. A wheel and _____ is a simple machine. A _ _ _ _

3. A _____ is a compound machine. C _ _ _

4. Friction makes _____. H _ _ _

5. A ramp is an _____ plane. I _ _ _ _ _ _ _

6. Every machine _____ energy. N _ _ _ _

7. A machine cannot make _____. E _ _ _ _ _

8. There are six kinds of _____ machines. S _ _ _ _ _

9. Pistons move up and _____. D _ _ _

10. Hot gases rush _____ of a jet plane's engine. O _ _

11. A _____ is a simple machine. W _ _ _ _

12. Each cylinder has its _____ spark plug. O _ _

13. Friction _____ motion. R _ _ _ _ _ _

14. Each _____ of lever has a fulcrum. K _ _ _

Just for Fun

Fill in the missing words in each sentence. Use the words below.

CDs	light	robot
Earth	machine	signal
laser	program	system

1. Because a computer cannot think, it must have instructions called a   _ _ _ _ _ _ _ .

9

2. A machine that can do tasks by itself is called a   _ _ _ _ _ .

6 8

3. A machine that makes light that is stronger than natural light is called a   _ _ _ _ _ .

7 2

4. All computers need an operating   _ _ _ _ _ _ .

10

5. Communications satellites orbit   _ _ _ _ _ .

1

6. Lasers are sometimes used to burn signals into   _ _ _ .

3

7. A laser sends a narrow beam of   _ _ _ _ _ .

4

8. You can send printed material on a fax   _ _ _ _ _ _ .

5

Solve the Secret Message. When a letter of a word above has a number under it, write that letter above the same number in the Secret Message.

Secret Message: Your life is easier because of

_ _ _ _ _ _ _ _ _ _ .

1 2 3 4 5 6 7 8 9 10

UNIT 1 Just for Fun

Fill in the missing words in each sentence. Use the words below.

atomic	gravity	mass	table
charges	leaf	metals	weight
element	liquid	solid	

1. Elements that are shiny and conduct heat are $\underset{14}{M}\ \underset{}{E}\ \underset{}{T}\ \underset{}{A}\ \underset{}{L}\ \underset{7}{S}$.

2. How much matter an object has is its $\underset{}{M}\ \underset{}{A}\ \underset{}{S}\ \underset{10}{S}$.

3. The number of protons in the nucleus of an atom of an element is its $\underset{18}{A}\ \underset{5}{T}\ \underset{}{O}\ \underset{17}{M}\ \underset{}{I}\ \underset{}{C}$ number.

4. The force that pulls matter toward the ground is $\underset{}{G}\ \underset{6}{R}\ \underset{}{A}\ \underset{}{V}\ \underset{}{I}\ \underset{20}{T}\ \underset{}{Y}$.

5. The simplest form of matter is an $\underset{21}{E}\ \underset{}{L}\ \underset{}{E}\ \underset{11}{M}\ \underset{}{E}\ \underset{}{N}\ \underset{}{T}$.

6. The pull of gravity on an object is the object's $\underset{4}{W}\ \underset{}{E}\ \underset{}{I}\ \underset{}{G}\ \underset{}{H}\ \underset{19}{T}$.

7. Elements are organized in a periodic $\underset{1}{T}\ \underset{12}{A}\ \underset{}{B}\ \underset{3}{L}\ \underset{}{E}$.

8. Electrons have negative $\underset{2}{C}\ \underset{}{H}\ \underset{}{A}\ \underset{}{R}\ \underset{}{G}\ \underset{}{E}\ \underset{22}{S}$.

9. A brick is a $\underset{15}{S}\ \underset{}{O}\ \underset{}{L}\ \underset{}{I}\ \underset{8}{D}$.

10. The metal gold can be made into sheets of gold $\underset{}{L}\ \underset{}{E}\ \underset{}{A}\ \underset{16}{F}$.

11. Milk is a $\underset{9}{L}\ \underset{}{I}\ \underset{}{Q}\ \underset{}{U}\ \underset{}{I}\ \underset{13}{D}$.

Solve the Secret Message. When a letter of a word above has a number under it, write that letter above the same number in the Secret Message.

Secret Message:

$\underset{1}{T}\ \underset{2}{H}\ \underset{3}{E}\quad \underset{4}{W}\ \underset{5}{O}\ \underset{6}{R}\ \underset{7}{L}\ \underset{8}{D}\quad \underset{9}{I}\ \underset{10}{S}\quad \underset{11}{M}\ \underset{12}{A}\ \underset{13}{D}\ \underset{14}{E}\quad \underset{15}{O}\ \underset{16}{F}\quad \underset{17}{M}\ \underset{18}{A}\ \underset{19}{T}\ \underset{20}{T}\ \underset{21}{E}\ \underset{22}{R}$

UNIT 2 Just for Fun

Use the clues to complete the puzzle. Choose from the words below.

acids	chemical	liquid	salt
ashes	energy	medicine	solution
bases	heat	rust	water

Across

3. When wood burns, it turns into smoke and this.
6. Lemonade is an example of this kind of mixture.
8. H_2O is the formula for this.
10. This helps your body fight disease.
11. A solid and a gas can both become this.

Down

1. These are compounds that feel soapy and slippery and have molecules with a negative electric charge.
2. Baking causes this kind of change.
4. Iron atoms join with oxygen atoms to form molecules of this new substance.
5. In a chemical change, this causes the atoms to break free of their molecules and form different molecules.
7. This can make water evaporate to become steam.
9. These are compounds that taste sour and have molecules with a positive electric charge.

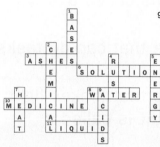

UNIT 3 Just for Fun

Each sentence below is about a source of energy. But one word in each sentence is scrambled. Unscramble the letters. Then write the correct word on the lines at the right. Choose from the words below. The first one is done for you.

atom	gasoline	oil	steam
electric	live	radiation	water
energy	nuclear	rivers	years

1. METSA is made in a boiler. **S T E A M**

2. Someday the supply of coal, LIO, and gasoline will run out. **O I L**

3. Nothing on Earth could IVLE without the sun. **L I V E**

4. When the nucleus of an MOTA splits, it gives off a very large amount of energy. **A T O M**

5. Dams are built on SERVIR and lakes. **R I V E R S**

6. Many large CRILETEC power plants have steam turbines. **E L E C T R I C**

7. Many people think that RENCULA energy is too dangerous to use. **N U C L E A R**

8. There are several kinds of YENGER. **E N E R G Y**

9. Heat from the sun comes to you in TORADINIA waves. **R A D I A T I O N**

10. NIGOLASE has chemical energy stored in it. **G A S O L I N E**

11. Coal and oil were formed from plants and animals millions of RESAY ago. **Y E A R S**

Solve the Secret Message. Find the first letters of all the words that you unscrambled and write them in order on the lines below.

Secret Message: The most important kind of energy is

$\underset{1}{S}\ \underset{2}{O}\ \underset{3}{L}\ \underset{4}{A}\ \underset{5}{R}\quad \underset{6}{E}\ \underset{7}{N}\ \underset{8}{E}\ \underset{9}{R}\ \underset{10}{G}\ \underset{11}{Y}$

UNIT 4 Just for Fun

Choose from the words below to answer the questions.

bend	energy	music	vocal
crest	iris	pitch	waves
eardrum	lenses	trough	

1. What part of your ear vibrates? $\underset{}{E}\ \underset{}{A}\ \underset{}{R}\ \underset{}{D}\ \underset{}{R}\ \underset{}{U}\ \underset{8}{M}$

2. What kind of sound is made of notes? $\underset{}{M}\ \underset{}{U}\ \underset{3}{S}\ \underset{}{I}\ \underset{}{C}$

3. What is the lowest part of a wave? $\underset{13}{T}\ \underset{}{R}\ \underset{}{O}\ \underset{}{U}\ \underset{2}{G}\ \underset{}{H}$

4. What is the colored part of your eye? $\underset{10}{I}\ \underset{}{R}\ \underset{}{I}\ \underset{1}{S}$

5. What is based on the frequency of a sound's waves? $\underset{}{P}\ \underset{}{I}\ \underset{}{T}\ \underset{}{C}\ \underset{12}{H}$

6. How do sound and light move? $\underset{}{W}\ \underset{}{A}\ \underset{}{V}\ \underset{6}{E}\ \underset{}{S}$

7. What do lenses do to light rays? $\underset{}{B}\ \underset{}{E}\ \underset{4}{N}\ \underset{5}{D}$

8. What cords vibrate when you talk? $\underset{}{V}\ \underset{}{O}\ \underset{}{C}\ \underset{}{A}\ \underset{9}{L}$

9. What are used in microscopes? $\underset{}{L}\ \underset{}{E}\ \underset{}{N}\ \underset{7}{S}\ \underset{}{E}\ \underset{}{S}$

10. What is light, music or energy? $\underset{}{E}\ \underset{}{N}\ \underset{}{E}\ \underset{}{R}\ \underset{}{G}\ \underset{11}{Y}$

Now find the letters that have numbers below them. Write those letters below. When you are finished, you will have the answer to a riddle.

Riddle: What kinds of energy move in waves?

$\underset{1}{S}\ \underset{2}{O}\ \underset{3}{U}\ \underset{4}{N}\ \underset{5}{D}\quad \underset{6}{A}\ \underset{7}{N}\ \underset{8}{D}\quad \underset{9}{L}\ \underset{10}{I}\ \underset{11}{G}\ \underset{12}{H}\ \underset{13}{T}$

UNIT 5 · Just for Fun

Use the clues to solve the puzzle. Use the words below.

another	electricity	lift	rid
atom	good	magnetism	safely
charged	iron	one	terminals
compasses			

Across

1. The north pole of one magnet attracts the south pole of _____ magnet.
4. An electromagnet can _____ tons of iron.
6. When electrons leave their atoms, matter becomes electrically _____.
7. The force that magnets have is _____.
9. As long as an _____ has the same number of protons and electrons, the atom has no charge.
10. An electromagnet has an _____ bar inside a coil of wire.
12. It is important to use electricity _____.

Down

2. The electric outlets in your house provide alternating current _____.
3. An atom that loses, or gets _____ of electrons, has a positive charge.
5. A dry cell has two posts called _____.
6. Sailors use _____ to tell which direction they are going.
8. Rubber is a _____ insulator.
11. A magnet has a north pole at _____ end and a south pole at the other end.

Crossword solution:
- 1 Across: ANOTHER
- 4 Across: LIFT
- Across: CHARGED
- MAGNETISM
- 9 ATOM
- 10 IRON
- 12 SAFELY
- Down words include: ELECTRICITY, COMPASSES, TERMINALS, GOOD, RID, ONE

T24

UNIT 6 · Just for Fun

Each sentence below is about motion and forces. But one word in each sentence is scrambled. Unscramble the letters. Then write the correct word on the spaces at the right. Choose from the words below. The first one is done for you.

differ	lift	speeds
force	motion	time
gravity	never	velocity

1. Any push or pull is a COFER.
   F O R C E
   (1, 15)

2. YETCOVIL is speed in a certain direction.
   V E L O C I T Y
   (9, 6)

3. Speed is the distance something moves in a certain MITE.
   T I M E
   (4, 11)

4. Forces FIDREF in size and direction.
   D I F F E R
   (10, 13, 2)

5. Powerful engines are needed to FLIT rockets into space.
   L I F T
   (7)

6. VAYTRIG attracts matter.
   G R A V I T Y
   (8, 3)

7. An object at rest will VEREN move if balanced forces act on it.
   N E V E R
   (14, 12)

8. It is positive acceleration if a car DESEPS up.
   S P E E D S
   (16, 5)

Solve the Secret Message. When a letter of a word above has a number under it, write that letter above the same number in the Secret Message.

Secret Message: To tell if something is in motion, you need a

F R A M E   O F   R E F E R E N C E .
1 2 3 4 5   6 7   8 9 10 11 12 13 14 15 16

T25

UNIT 7 · Just for Fun

The following sentences are about machines. But one word is missing in each sentence. Write in the missing words on the spaces at the right. Choose from the words below. The first letter of each missing word is written in for you. Read the letters down the first column for a message about machines.

axle	energy	move	resists
car	heat	needs	simple
complex	inclined	out	wedge
down	kind	own	

1. To do work, a force must _____ something. **M** O V E
2. A wheel and _____ is a simple machine. **A** X L E
3. A _____ is a compound machine. **C** A R
4. Friction makes _____. **H** E A T
5. A ramp is an _____ plane. **I** N C L I N E D
6. Every machine _____ energy. **N** E E D S
7. A machine cannot make _____. **E** N E R G Y
8. There are six kinds of _____ machines. **S** I M P L E
9. Pistons move up and _____. **D** O W N
10. Hot gases rush _____ of a jet plane's engine. **O** U T
11. A _____ is a simple machine. **W** E D G E
12. Each cylinder has its _____ spark plug. **O** W N
13. Friction _____ motion. **R** E S I S T S
14. Each _____ of lever has a fulcrum. **K** I N D

T26

UNIT 8 · Just for Fun

Fill in the missing words in each sentence. Use the words below.

CDs	light	robot
Earth	machine	signal
laser	program	system

1. Because a computer cannot think, it must have instructions called a
   P R O G R A M
   (9)

2. A machine that can do tasks by itself is called a
   R O B O T
   (6, 8)

3. A machine that makes light that is stronger than natural light is called a
   L A S E R
   (7, 2)

4. All computers need an operating
   S Y S T E M
   (10)

5. Communications satellites orbit
   E A R T H
   (1)

6. Lasers are sometimes used to burn signals into
   C D s
   (3)

7. A laser sends a narrow beam of
   L I G H T
   (4)

8. You can send printed material on a fax
   M A C H I N E
   (5)

Solve the Secret Message. When a letter of a word above has a number under it, write that letter above the same number in the Secret Message.

Secret Message: Your life is easier because of

T E C H N O L O G Y
1 2 3 4 5 6 7 8 9 10

T27

T29

Special Projects

These Special Projects are motivational activities that supplement and provide enrichment to each unit. Read through the projects before beginning a unit to determine when each is most helpful to your class.

UNIT 1 Matter

Four Elements Guessing Game
Materials: periodic table

Invite students to try a guessing game. Four little-known elements were discovered near a small town in Sweden called Ytterby. Tell students to consult a full periodic table of elements. Who can guess from their names which four elements were named for Ytterby? (erbium, terbium, ytterbium, and yttrium)

Research on Elements
Materials: encyclopedia

Have students choose a metal, a nonmetal, a metalloid, or an inert gas from the periodic table and research it in the library. Ask them to learn where the element is found, what special properties it has, and what products are manufactured with it.

UNIT 2 Changes in Matter

Making and Separating Mixtures
Materials: sand, salt, water, two small jars, stirrer, filter paper, paper towel

Mix sand and salt on a paper towel. Ask students if they can think of a way to separate the salt from the sand. Pour the mixture into a jar, fill the jar with water, and stir until the salt dissolves. Put filter paper over the mouth of a second jar and pour the salt solution through the paper. The sand remains on the filter paper. Ask how the salt can be retrieved from the water. Let the solution sit in the air for several days. After the water has evaporated, the salt will appear as a white crust in the jar.

Identifying Acids and Bases
Materials: vinegar, orange juice, milk, water, aspirin tablet, antacid tablet, five small jars, red and blue litmus paper

Place vinegar, orange juice, and milk in separate jars. Crush the tablets, put the powder in separate jars, and dissolve each powder in water. Have students test all five liquids with both types of litmus paper. Make a chart that lists each substance and the color change of the red or the blue litmus paper.

UNIT 3 Nature's Energies

Testing Whether Hot Air Rises
Materials: empty soda bottle, balloon, hot water, pan

Place the open end of a balloon over the mouth of the empty soda bottle. Put the bottle in a pan of hot water. Ask students to observe what happens to the balloon. (It will blow up slightly.) Ask students why this happened. (The air in the bottle was warmed by the hot water and expanded into the balloon.)

The Power of Water
Materials: pitcher of water, dry soil, pebbles, basin

In a basin, shape a small mound of soil and pebbles. Gently pour water on the mound. The water will first form a hole in the mound and then carve small indentations as it runs down the sides of the mound, carrying pebbles along. Explain that over millions of years, the power of moving water has shaped the face of Earth in much the same way as it changed the mound.

UNIT 4 Sound and Light

Changing Noise into Music
Materials: desk, metal ruler

Rest a metal ruler at the end of a desk, extending most of it over the edge. Hold the ruler firmly and pluck the other end. The vibrations will make a noise. Move the ruler so less of it extends over the edge, then pluck it. Keep moving the ruler until only a few inches extend over the desk. As the plucked part of the ruler gets shorter, the sound it makes becomes more musical because the vibrations are more regular. Also, the pitch becomes higher because the ruler vibrates faster.

Light Charts

Have students list on paper seven objects in the classroom. Beside each item on the list, students should write a one-sentence description of the object and state whether it absorbs, reflects, or refracts light. For example: "A pair of scissors is shiny. It reflects light. The chalkboard is black. It absorbs light."

UNIT 5 Magnetism and Electricity

Static Electricity

Materials: plastic comb, nylon cloth, paper

Tear paper into tiny pieces. Rub a comb with a nylon cloth. Place the comb into the pile of paper bits. The paper pieces will cling briefly to the comb. Rubbing the comb with the cloth rubs electrons off the cloth onto the comb, giving the comb a negative charge. At first, the negatively charged comb pushes electrons on the paper to the far side of the paper, away from the comb. The positively charged paper clings to the comb (unlike charges attract). Soon, the negative charge on the paper builds up, and the paper falls from the comb (like charges repel).

Research on the History of Science

Materials: encyclopedia

Have students research the lives of some of the pioneers in the discovery of electricity and magnetism (for example, Benjamin Franklin, Hans Christian Oersted, Andre Ampere, Michael Faraday, Joseph Henry, and Nikola Tesla).

UNIT 6 Motion and Forces

Observing a Law of Motion and Gravity

Materials: stiff paper, scissors, tape, drinking glass, coin

Cut a strip of stiff paper about one inch wide and eight inches long. Roll the strip into a hoop and tape it closed. Place the hoop on top of an empty glass so it balances there, dipping somewhat into the mouth of the glass. Place a coin on top of the hoop. Tell students to watch the coin carefully. Quickly pull the hoop from under the coin. The coin will remain in midair for a discernible moment. Then it will fall into the glass. Ask why the coin seemed to "hesitate" before falling. In terms of Newton's first law of motion: A body in motion tends to remain in motion; a body at rest tends to remain at rest. But a moment after the forces become unbalanced, gravity takes over and pulls the coin down.

Research on the History of Science

Materials: encyclopedia

Have students work in pairs to research the life of Isaac Newton or the history of space travel. If the former project is chosen, suggest to students that they find out when and where Newton lived and some information about scientific beliefs at that time. If the latter project is chosen, students might develop a chart of milestones in space travel.

UNIT 7 Machines

Friction Charts

Have students work in pairs and create friction charts in which they list five common activities where friction is desirable and five activities where decreased friction is wanted. For example, driving a car is an activity where friction is desirable; ice skating is an activity where reduced friction is desirable.

Research on Machines/Technical Drawing

Materials: encyclopedia, books on machines, drawing paper, marking pens

Have students choose a machine that interests them and research how it works. Students should make a drawing of their machine, labeling its major parts. Students may want to choose a machine they have at home, such as a bicycle, or a simple machine, such as a screwdriver.

UNIT 8 Technology

Research on the History of Science

Materials: encyclopedia

Have students research the history of computer technology. They may be surprised to learn how huge and cumbersome the first computers were. The first American computer, ENIAC, was built in 1946 and filled an entire large room.

A Wish List: Future Technologies

Have students work in pairs to compose a "wish list" of areas in which they would like to see advances in technology. Have them consider problems, such as pollution and food shortages, and imagine technologies that could solve some problems.

Related Harcourt Achieve Products

Additional resources are available from Harcourt Achieve to enrich the content of *Matter, Motion, and Machines*. Many of the titles are available in hard cover or soft cover. Readability range is from 4th to 6th grade level.

Raintree Illustrated Science Encyclopedia

20 Events Series
Transportation Milestones and Breakthroughs

Breakthrough Series
Electricity

Exploring Music Series
Brass
Keyboards and Electronic Music
Percussion
Strings
Woodwinds

Facing the Future Series
Renewable Energy
Transportation

How Do We Know? Series
Energy Exists
How to Measure

Visual FactFinder Series
Science and Technology

Rigby • Steck-Vaughn

For ordering information call
Harcourt Achieve customer service
1-800-531-5015.

Steck Vaughn

WONDERS OF SCIENCE

Matter, Motion, and Machines

Joan S. Gottlieb

ISBN 0-7398-9179-0

1 2 3 4 5 6 7 8 862 11 10 09 08 07 06 05 04

Harcourt Achieve
Rigby • Steck-Vaughn

www.HarcourtAchieve.com
1.800.531.5015

Contents

UNIT 1
Matter

What Is Matter?

What do water, a rock, and a dog have in common? They are all made of **matter.** You are made of matter. Everything you see or touch is matter. The whole world around you is made of matter.

Matter is anything that takes up space and has **mass.** What is mass? Mass is a measure of how much matter an object has. For example, a mountain takes up space and has mass. A rock takes up space and has mass. A mountain has more mass than a rock. But they are both matter. A kitten has less mass than a tiger. But they are both matter.

On Earth, mass seems about the same as weight. But in space we can see they are different. Astronauts have the same mass on Earth and in space. In space, the pull of gravity is so little that they float in their spacecraft. Weight is the pull of **gravity** upon a body or object.

Gravity is a <u>force</u>. The gravity of Earth pulls on all matter near Earth. Gravity pulls matter toward the ground. Gravity is why anything you drop falls to the ground. Without gravity, you would float in the air.

Gravity is strongest at the center of Earth. Far from the center, at the top of a mountain, gravity is weaker. Suppose you were in a deep hole in Earth. Gravity would be strong. It would pull hard on you. So you would weigh more than you would weigh on top of a mountain. Farther from Earth's center, gravity does not pull as hard.

Different Types of Matter

A. Answer True or False.

1. You are made of matter. _____True_____

2. A kitten is not made of matter. _____False_____

3. Matter is anything that takes up space and has mass. _____True_____

4. In space, mass is the same as weight. _____False_____

5. Weight is the pull of gravity upon an object. _____True_____

6. Gravity is the strongest at the center of Earth. _____True_____

7. Farther from Earth's center, gravity pulls harder. _____False_____

B. Write the letter for the correct answer.

1. Anything that takes up space and has mass is _____b_____.
   (a) gravity   (b) matter   (c) weight

2. The pull that gravity has on an object is the object's _____b_____.
   (a) space   (b) weight   (c) mass

3. Everything you see or touch is _____c_____.
   (a) gravity   (b) weight   (c) matter

4. Gravity is _____a_____ at the center of Earth.
   (a) strongest   (b) hottest   (c) weakest

5. Matter is pulled to the ground by _____c_____.
   (a) space   (b) air   (c) gravity

C. Remember that gravity is strongest at the center of Earth. For each pair of places, write X where the weight of an object would be greater.

1. down in a deep hole _____X_____

   on top of a mountain _____

2. in an airplane in the air _____

   in an airport on the ground _____X_____

3. in a spaceship about to take off from the launching pad _____X_____

   in a spaceship traveling in outer space _____

5

States of Matter

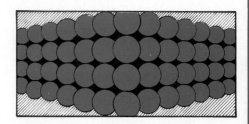

Solid

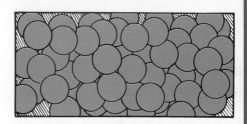

Liquid

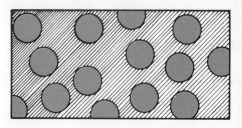

Gas

Plasma

A brick, milk, steam, and lightning are all matter. But they are in different **states**. Matter can exist in four states. Matter can be **solid**, like a brick. It can be **liquid**, like milk. It can be a **gas**, like steam. Or it can be **plasma**, like lightning.

All matter is made of tiny particles. These particles are always moving. Heat makes them move faster. And heat usually makes the particles move farther apart.

In a solid the particles are usually packed close together. They are in a pattern. This gives a solid a shape. The particles in a solid can only jiggle. They can't move around each other. Ice is a solid.

If you heat ice, it will become a liquid. It will become water. The heat makes the particles move around. They can slide past each other. A liquid does not have its own shape. It takes the shape of its container. A liquid has mass. It fills up space. You see this when a container is filled with water or another liquid.

Heat makes water evaporate. The water becomes a gas. In a gas the particles are far apart. They move faster than in a liquid. They bounce around and even hit each other. A gas has no shape of its own. A gas can fill space. You see this when a balloon is filled with air. Air is a gas.

Adding a lot of heat to a gas changes it. The particles themselves separate. This is called plasma.

Most of the matter in the universe is plasma. The sun and most of the stars you see are plasma. But plasma is a state of matter that is not common on Earth.

A. Write the letter for the correct answer.

1. A liquid takes the shape of its ___a___.
   (a) container   (b) pattern   (c) plasma

2. The particles in a liquid ___b___.
   (a) are held very close together   (b) can move around
   (c) cannot move

3. Steam is a ___c___.
   (a) solid   (b) liquid   (c) gas

4. A brick is ___b___.
   (a) plasma   (b) solid   (c) liquid

5. In a solid, the particles are packed together in a ___a___.
   (a) pattern   (b) plasma   (c) gas

6. In a gas, the particles are very ___c___.
   (a) close together   (b) slow moving   (c) far apart

B. Answer True or False.

1. Solid, liquid, gas, and plasma are the states of matter. ___True___

2. Matter can be solid like a brick. ___True___

3. Adding heat to a gas can make particles separate. ___True___

4. Heat makes water evaporate. ___True___

5. In a solid, the particles are far apart from one another. ___False___

6. The particles in a liquid cannot move around. ___False___

7. Solids do not have any certain shape. ___False___

C. List the four states of matter. Write an example of each state.

1. ___solid___   example: ___Answers will vary.___

2. ___liquid___   example: _____

3. ___gas___   example: _____

4. ___plasma___   example: _____

Atoms

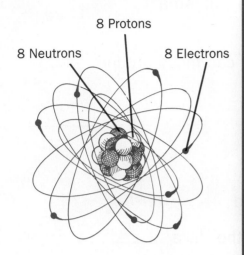

8 Neutrons

8 Protons

8 Electrons

An oxygen atom has 8 positive protons and 8 neutrons in its nucleus, and 8 negative electrons speeding around the nucleus.

Everything is made of **atoms.** Atoms are tiny pieces of matter. They are too small to see even under a microscope. In fact, the smallest piece of matter you can see under a microscope has 10 billion atoms.

Atoms are made of even tinier bits of matter. There are three kinds of particles in atoms. They are **protons, neutrons,** and **electrons.** All electrons are exactly the same. All protons are alike, too. So are all neutrons. If all atoms are made of the same kinds of particles, how are atoms different?

Different kinds of atoms are different from each other because they contain a different number of particles. A carbon atom has six protons, six neutrons, and six electrons. Oxygen has eight protons, eight neutrons, and eight electrons. Oxygen is different from carbon because it has more particles. Each kind of atom has a different number of the three particles.

Protons and neutrons are in the center, or **nucleus,** of the atom. Electrons are much smaller than protons and neutrons. Electrons move around the nucleus at great speeds. Because electrons move so fast, it is impossible to tell exactly where an electron is at any one time.

The particles that are in atoms have different **electric charges.** Electrons have a negative electric charge. Protons have a positive electric charge. Neutrons have no electric charge. An atom with the same number of electrons and protons also has no electric charge. An atom without an electric charge is called a neutral atom.

Draw lines to complete the sentences.

1. Atoms — have a positive electric charge.

2. Electrons — are made of protons, neutrons, and electrons.

3. Neutrons — have a negative electric charge.

4. Protons — have no electric charge.

5. The nucleus ———— is made of protons and neutrons.

B. **Write the letter for the correct answer.**

1. Atoms are made of three small ____b____.
   (a) elements   (b) particles   (c) electrons

2. All electrons are ____a____.
   (a) exactly the same   (b) positive   (c) different

3. Different kinds of atoms are different from each other because they contain a different ____b____ of particles.
   (a) size   (b) number   (c) speed

4. Protons and neutrons are in the center, or ____a____, of the atom.
   (a) nucleus   (b) electron   (c) charge

5. Protons have ____b____.
   (a) negative charges   (b) positive charges   (c) no charge

6. Because electrons ____c____, it is impossible to tell exactly where an electron is at any one time.
   (a) move too slowly   (b) do not move   (c) move so fast

7. Neutrons have ____c____.
   (a) positive charges   (b) negative charges
   (c) no electric charge

C. **Use each word to write a sentence about the parts of an atom.**

1. proton _____ Sentences will vary. _____

   _____

2. electron _____

   _____

9

Elements

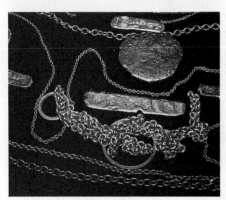

The iron in the gate, the gold in the jewelry, and the hydrogen and oxygen in the water are all elements.

Elements are the simplest form of matter. An element is matter that is made of only one kind of atom. All the atoms of an element are exactly the same. Gold is an element. All the atoms in a bar of gold are the same. Oxygen is also an element. Every oxygen atom is exactly the same. But oxygen atoms are very different from gold atoms.

Because elements are made of only one kind of atom, they cannot be broken down into different <u>substances</u>. No matter how tiny you cut an element, it will still be the element. One atom of gold is still gold.

You can think of an element as being like sand. Grains of sand are like the atoms in an element. The grains are all alike. You can separate sand any way you like, but it is still sand. Even a single grain of sand is still sand.

Every element is different from all other elements. Atoms of one element have a different number of particles than atoms of every other element. Only oxygen atoms have eight of each particle. Every other element has a different number.

Most elements are found in nature. Iron is an element that is found inside Earth. Wrought iron gates, fireplace grates, and bathtubs are made of iron. Gold is also an element that is found on Earth. Jewelry is often made of gold.

Some matter is made of more than one element. The air you breathe is oxygen, <u>nitrogen</u>, and other elements. Water is made of the elements hydrogen and oxygen. All matter is made of elements.

A. Fill in the missing words.

1. Elements are the simplest form of _____matter_____. (iron, matter)

2. An element is matter that is made of only one kind of _____atom_____. (atom, sand)

3. Every element is _____different from_____ all other elements. (different from, the same as)

4. Elements _____cannot_____ be broken down into different substances. (can, cannot)

5. Fireplace grates and bathtubs are made of the element _____iron_____. (gold, iron)

6. The air you breathe is _____more than one_____ element. (one, more than one)

7. All matter is made of _____elements_____. (elements, sand)

8. Atoms of one element have a different _____number_____ of particles than atoms of every other element. (kind, number)

B. Make a list of at least three elements.

_____Answers will vary,_____

_____but should include: oxygen, gold, iron, nitrogen,_____

_____and hydrogen._____

C. Answer True or False.

1. Elements are the simplest form of matter. _____True_____

2. An element is made of many different kinds of atoms. _____False_____

3. Every element is the same as every other element. _____False_____

4. Elements can be broken down into other substances. _____False_____

5. Iron and gold are elements. _____True_____

6. Oxygen is one of the elements in air. _____True_____

7. Some matter is made of more than one element. _____True_____

8. Water is made of the elements iron and gold. _____False_____

Metals

There are more than 110 elements. Most of the elements are **metals.** You see metals around you every day. Gold and silver are metals. So is iron.

All metals have some things in common. They are all shiny. Light bounces off metal surfaces and makes them gleam. For this reason, metals are often used for decoration.

Metals **conduct** heat. Heat passes easily through metal and into other objects. That is why pots for cooking are made of metals.

Metals also conduct electricity. Electricity passes through metal easily. In addition, metals are **ductile,** or easily shaped into a new form. This means that they can be pulled into a thin wire. Because metals are ductile and conduct electricity, wire made of metals such as copper is used to carry electricity.

Many metals are easy to shape. They can be made into jewelry. Aluminum can be made into thin sheets of aluminum foil. Gold can be made into thin sheets of gold leaf. The torch of the Statue of Liberty is covered with gold leaf.

There are even metals in your body. Calcium and magnesium are metals that help make your bones. Sodium is a metal that your body needs to work properly. There is sodium in table salt.

People have found thousands of uses for metals. We buy things with coins made of metal. We travel in cars, trains, and planes made of metal. We use tools and machines made of metal. Metals are part of our daily lives.

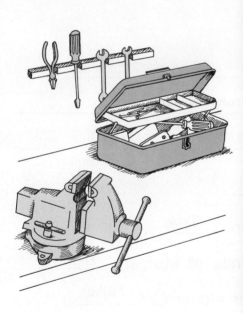

Things made of metal are everywhere.

A. **Fill in the missing words.**

1. Most of the elements are ____metals____. (metals, iron)

2. Metals are ____shiny____. (shiny, black)

3. Metals ____conduct____ heat and electricity. (stop, conduct)

4. Metals can be pulled _____into thin wire_____.
   (apart, into thin wire)

5. Gold and aluminum can be made into _____thin sheets_____.
   (sodium, thin sheets)

6. Calcium and magnesium are metals that help make your ____bones____.
   (hair, bones)

7. People have found thousands of uses for ____metals____.
   (sodium, metals)

B. **Answer True or False.**

1. There is sodium in table salt. ____True____

2. Metals are not shiny. ____False____

3. Metals conduct heat and electricity. ____True____

4. Metals cannot be pulled into thin wire. ____False____

5. Gold can be made into thin sheets called gold leaf. ____True____

6. Your body does not have metals in it. ____False____

C. **Write M after statements that describe metals.**

1. They are black. _____

2. Electricity will not pass through them. _____

3. They are shiny. ____M____

4. They can be pulled into a thin wire. ____M____

5. They let heat pass through them. ____M____

6. People have not found many uses for them. _____

Metalloids, Nonmetals, and Inert Gases

The metalloid silicon is part of the substance that makes up sand.

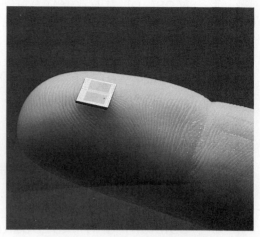

Silicon is used to make the tiny chips that make computers run.

A small number of the elements are not metals. These elements are divided into three types: **metalloids, nonmetals,** and **inert gases.**

Metalloids are elements that are like metals in some ways. They are shiny like metals. But they do not conduct heat and electricity as well as metals do. Silicon is a metalloid. Sand is made mostly of silicon. There is silicon in glass. The chips that make computers work are also made of silicon.

Nonmetals are not like metals at all. They are not shiny. They do not conduct heat or electricity well. They cannot be used to make wire. Nonmetals can be solids, liquids, or gases. Carbon is a solid nonmetal. Diamonds are made of carbon that has been squeezed together underground. Carbon is one of the elements that forms your body. Bromine is a liquid nonmetal. Small amounts of bromine are in seawater. Oxygen and nitrogen are nonmetals that are gases. The air you breathe is made up mostly of oxygen and nitrogen.

Inert gases won't by themselves combine to form a different gas. There are only six kinds of these gases. Helium is a lightweight inert gas. It is used in balloons.

A. Fill in the missing words.

1. A __small__ number of the elements are not metals. (small, large)

2. Silicon is a __metalloid__. (gas, metalloid)

3. Nonmetals are not like __metals__ at all. (metals, liquids)

4. Diamonds are made of __carbon__. (sand, carbon)

5. Bromine is a __liquid__ nonmetal. (liquid, solid)

6. Oxygen and nitrogen are two nonmetals that are __gases__. (shiny, gases)

7. Helium is __an inert gas__. (an inert gas, a metal)

B. Answer True or False.

1. All elements are metals. __False__

2. Metalloids are shiny. __True__

3. Metalloids conduct heat and electricity just as well as metals do.
__False__

4. Nonmetals can be solids, liquids, or gases. __True__

5. Carbon is a nonmetal. __True__

6. Air is made up mostly of oxygen and nitrogen. __True__

7. Inert gases, such as helium, easily combine together to form a
different gas. __False__

8. Silicon is an inert gas used in balloons. __False__

C. Draw lines to complete the sentences.

1. Helium ⟍ is a nonmetal that is a gas.

2. Oxygen ⟋ is an inert gas.

3. Bromine ——— is a liquid nonmetal.

4. Nonmetals ——— are not like metals at all.

5. Metalloids ——— are like metals in some ways.

Periodic Table

Part of the Periodic Table, Through Atomic Number 54

I	II												III	IV	V	VI	VII	VIII

atomic number ——— 8

symbol of element ——— O

element name ——— Oxygen

Elements above and to the right of this line are nonmetals.

Elements below and to the left of this line are metals.

1 **H** Hydrogen																		2 **He** Helium
3 **Li** Lithium	4 **Be** Beryllium												5 **B** Boron	6 **C** Carbon	7 **N** Nitrogen	8 **O** Oxygen	9 **F** Fluorine	10 **Ne** Neon
11 **Na** Sodium	12 **Mg** Magnesium												13 **Al** Aluminum	14 **Si** Silicon	15 **P** Phosphorus	16 **S** Sulfur	17 **Cl** Chlorine	18 **Ar** Argon
19 **K** Potassium	20 **Ca** Calcium	21 **SC** Scandium	22 **Ti** Titanium	23 **V** Vanadium	24 **Cr** Chromium	25 **Mn** Manganese	26 **Fe** Iron	27 **Co** Cobalt	28 **Ni** Nickel	29 **Cu** Copper	30 **Zn** Zinc	31 **Ga** Gallium	32 **Ge** Germanium	33 **As** Arsenic	34 **Se** Selenium	35 **Br** Bromine	36 **Kr** Krypton
37 **Rb** Rubidium	38 **Sr** Strontium	39 **Y** Yttrium	40 **Zr** Zirconium	41 **Nb** Niobium	42 **Mo** Molybdenum	43 **Tc** Technetium	44 **Ru** Ruthenium	45 **Rh** Rhodium	46 **Pd** Palladium	47 **Ag** Silver	48 **Cd** Cadmium	49 **In** Indium	50 **Sn** Tin	51 **Sb** Antimony	52 **Te** Tellurium	53 **I** Iodine	54 **Xe** Xenon

Scientists have organized all the elements in a chart called the **periodic table.** It lists all of the elements in rows and columns. Elements similar to one another are in the same column. Scientists can tell a lot about an element from where it is found in the periodic table.

The elements are arranged in rows according to their **atomic numbers.** The atomic number of an element is the number of protons in the nucleus of one of its atoms. Oxygen has eight protons. The atomic number of oxygen is 8. No two elements have the same atomic number.

All elements in the periodic table have symbols. O is the symbol for oxygen. Na is the symbol for sodium. Scientists use these symbols in formulas. The formula for water is H_2O. The "H" stands for hydrogen. The "$_2$" means there are two hydrogen atoms for every oxygen atom.

Fill in the missing words.

1. No two elements have the same ___atomic___ number. (periodic, atomic)

2. Every element has a ___symbol___. (symbol, formula)

3. O is the symbol for ___oxygen___. (water, oxygen)

Part A

Fill in the missing words.

1. Everything you see or touch is ___matter___. (gas, matter)

2. Matter is anything that takes up space and has ___mass___. (oxygen, mass)

3. Matter can exist in four ___states___. (states, places)

4. Everything is made of ___atoms___. (carbon, atoms)

5. Atoms are different because they contain different ___numbers___ of particles. (numbers, colors)

6. Electrons are much ___smaller___ than protons and neutrons. (larger, smaller)

7. The simplest form of matter is ___an element___. (an element, liquid)

8. Elements cannot be ___broken down into___ other substances. (broken down into, mixed with)

9. Heat and electricity pass through ___metals___ easily. (inert gases, metals)

10. Elements are organized in the ___periodic___ table. (periodic, atomic)

Part B

Read each sentence. Write <u>True</u> if the sentence is True. Write <u>False</u> if the sentence is false.

1. Gravity makes anything you drop float in the air. ___False___

2. Weight is the pull of gravity upon a body or object. ___True___

3. Liquid matter takes the shape of the container you put it in. ___True___

4. Atoms are made up of electrons, protons, and neutrons. ___True___

5. Every electron is different from every other electron. ___False___

6. Elements are made up of many different kinds of atoms. ___False___

7. Nonmetals can be solids, liquids, or gases. ___True___

Investigate Particles in Liquids

You Need

- clear plastic cup
- water
- food coloring
- medicine dropper

1. Fill the plastic cup with water.

2. Set the cup on a flat table and wait until you can no longer see the water moving around.

3. Use the medicine dropper to pick up one drop of food coloring.

4. Stick the medicine dropper into the water and release the food coloring as shown in the picture.

5. Observe carefully. How does the liquid in the cup look at first? How does it look after a few minutes?

Write the Answer

What happened? What does this show about how particles move in a liquid?

The food coloring spread throughout the water

until all of the water was the same color. This shows that particles

in a liquid move about quickly and easily.

Fill in the circle in front of the word or phrase that best completes each sentence. The first one is done for you.

1. Anything that takes up space and has mass is
   - ⓐ a solid.
   - ● matter.
   - ⓒ an element.

2. How much matter an object has is its
   - ⓐ mass.
   - ⓑ atomic number.
   - ⓒ gravity.

3. Atoms are very
   - ⓐ heavy.
   - ⓑ tiny.
   - ⓒ large.

4. The pull of gravity upon a body or an object is called
   - ⓐ matter.
   - ⓑ mass.
   - ⓒ weight.

5. The particles in atoms have different
   - ⓐ electric charges.
   - ⓑ gases.
   - ⓒ flavors.

6. The formula for water is
   - ⓐ Na.
   - ⓑ O.
   - ⓒ H_2O.

Fill in the missing words.

7. Most elements are found in _____nature_____. (space, nature)

8. Most of the elements are _____metals_____. (metals, nonmetals)

9. Lightning is a kind of _____plasma_____. (liquid, plasma)

Write the answer on the lines.

10. How are the elements in the periodic table arranged?

_____The elements in the periodic table_____

_____are arranged according to their atomic number._____

19

UNIT 2 Changes in Matter

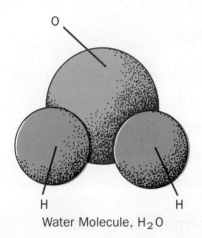

Water Molecule, H_2O

Water covers more than half of Earth's surface.

Molecules and Compounds

A **molecule** is a group of atoms. Most matter can be broken down into molecules. Elements are made of only one kind of atom. So the molecules of an element contain only one kind of atom.

A **compound** is a substance that is made from molecules of more than one element. Water is a compound. In Unit 1, you learned that the formula for water is H_2O. This formula means that there are two atoms of hydrogen and one atom of oxygen in each water molecule.

Atoms of different elements join together to form molecules of a compound. A new substance is formed. This substance differs from the elements it is made of.

An atom is the smallest bit of an element that is still that element. In the same way, a molecule is the smallest bit of a compound that is still that compound. A water molecule has two atoms of hydrogen and one atom of oxygen. But these atoms are not water until they combine to form a molecule.

Every molecule in a compound is exactly the same. The formula for a compound is like a recipe for one molecule of the compound. If you follow the recipe, you always come out with the same compound. Compounds form in different ways. Have you ever seen iron rust? It turns red-brown and forms flakes. Rust is a compound. When iron gets wet, it can combine with oxygen from the air to form the compound rust. The symbol for iron is Fe. The formula for rust is Fe_2O_3.

A. Fill in the missing words.

1. A molecule is a group of _____atoms_____. (atoms, formulas)

2. Most matter can be broken down into _____molecules_____. (compounds, molecules)

3. A compound is made from molecules of _____more than one_____ element. (one, more than one)

4. Water is a _____compound_____. (solid, compound)

5. A _____molecule_____ is the smallest bit of a compound that is still that compound. (molecule, substance)

6. Every molecule in a compound is _____exactly the same_____. (different, exactly the same)

7. When iron gets wet, it can combine with oxygen from the air to form the compound _____rust_____. (rust, water)

B. Answer True or False.

1. Most matter can be broken down into molecules. _____True_____

2. The formula for water is OH. _____False_____

3. When atoms of different elements form molecules of a compound, a new substance is formed. _____True_____

4. A molecule is the smallest bit of an element that is still that element. _____False_____

5. Rust is a compound. _____True_____

6. The formula for iron is Fe_2O_3. _____False_____

C. Draw lines to complete the sentences.

1. Compounds   is a group of atoms.

2. Water   are made of only one kind of atom.

3. Elements   is a compound.

4. A molecule   form in different ways.

Mixtures

Tuna salad is an example of a mixture.

Lemonade is an example of a solution.

Most of the things you see in everyday life are not pure elements or compounds. They are **mixtures** of different elements and compounds. Some mixtures happen in nature. People also mix elements and compounds to make many different things.

When elements and compounds combine together to form a mixture, no new substances are made. This is because no new molecules are formed. The molecules of the elements and compounds are just mixed together. Scientists can always separate a mixture back into the substances from which it was made.

Mixtures are not always the same. Air is a mixture. Air is different in different places. Air in cities or near factories is dirtier than air in the country. The air in a pine forest smells like pine trees. Air in different places has different molecules in it.

Sometimes you can tell that a substance is a mixture. For example, tuna salad is usually made of tuna, celery, and mayonnaise. You can still see the pieces of tuna and celery in the mixture. You can separate the tuna and the celery out of the tuna salad.

But what about lemonade? It is made of lemon juice and water and sugar, but it does not look like a mixture. It is not easy to separate back into its parts. This kind of mixture is called a **solution.** Most solutions are liquids, but some are solid. If you melted gold and silver and mixed them together and let the mixture harden, it would be a solid solution.

A. Use the words below to complete the sentences.

compound	molecules	separate
mixture	same	solid

1. When elements and compounds combine to form a

   _____mixture_____ , no new substances are made.

2. Scientists can always _____separate_____ a mixture back into the substances from which it was made.

3. Mixtures are not always the _____same_____ .

4. Air in different places has different _____molecules_____ in it.

5. Most solutions are liquids, but some are _____solid_____ .

B. Write the letter for the correct answer.

1. Most of the things you see in everyday life are ____b____ .
   (a) metals   (b) mixtures   (c) wood

2. When elements and compounds combine to form a mixture, no new

   ____c____ are made.
   (a) atoms   (b) liquids   (c) substances

3. Lemonade is an example of a ____b____ .
   (a) molecule   (b) solution   (c) compound

4. Most solutions are ____a____ .
   (a) liquids   (b) gases   (c) elements

C. Answer the questions.

1. Why are no new substances made when elements and compounds

   combine to form a mixture? ____No new molecules are formed.____

   _____

2. If you melted gold and silver and mixed them together and then

   let the mixture harden, what would it be? ____It would be a____

   ____solid solution.____

Physical Changes

Water boiling is a physical change.

Wood being sawed is also a physical change.

A **physical change** is any change in matter that does not change the matter's molecules. When any kind of mixture is formed, a physical change takes place. But the molecules that make the mixture do not change.

Another kind of physical change takes place when matter changes state. You know that three of the states of matter are solid, liquid, and gas. A solid or a gas can become a liquid. A liquid can become a solid or a gas. The state of matter depends mostly upon its temperature.

Heat makes molecules move faster. They move faster in liquids than in solids. They move faster in gases than in liquids. Heat also changes how molecules are held together. They are usually closer together in solids than in liquids. They are closer together in liquids than in gases. The amount of heat needed for a substance to change state is not the same for all matter. Water takes more heat to become a gas than many liquids do. Ice takes less heat to become a liquid than most solids. Can you name some other solids that can easily be melted, or made into liquids? What are some solids that would take a great amount of heat to melt?

A third kind of physical change takes place when there is a change in the shape of the substance. When you saw wood, some of it is changed into sawdust. The molecules in sawdust are the same as the molecules in the piece of wood. Only the shape of the wood has changed.

A. Underline the correct words.

1. A physical change is any change in matter that does not change the matter's (<u>molecules</u>, shape).

2. A physical change takes place when matter changes (color, <u>states</u>).

3. The state of matter depends mostly on its (molecules, <u>temperature</u>).

4. A solid or a gas can become (steam, <u>a liquid</u>).

5. Ice is a (gas, <u>solid</u>).

6. When you saw wood, you cause a (chemical, <u>physical</u>) change.

B. Answer True or False.

1. When mixtures are formed, a physical change takes place.
   <u>True</u>

2. A liquid cannot become a solid or a gas. <u>False</u>

3. Heat makes molecules move slower. <u>False</u>

4. The amount of heat needed for a substance to change state is not the same for all matter. <u>True</u>

5. A physical change takes place when you change the shape of a substance. <u>True</u>

6. The molecules in sawdust are different from the molecules in pieces of wood. <u>False</u>

C. Use each word to write a sentence about the physical changes in matter.

1. water _____ Sentences will vary. _____

   _____

2. wood _____

   _____

25

Chemical Changes

Burning wood is a chemical change.

Rusting iron is a chemical change.

A **chemical change** happens whenever there is a change in a substance's molecules. Chemical changes always make new substances. In a chemical change, energy causes the atoms to break free of their molecules and form different molecules.

Burning wood is a chemical change. Wood is changed into new substances—ashes and smoke. The energy of the fire causes the atoms in the wood molecules to break apart. The atoms then form into molecules of ash and smoke. Rusting iron is another chemical change. Iron atoms join with oxygen atoms to form molecules of a new substance. This new substance is rust.

Matter is never lost in a chemical change. There are always exactly the same number of atoms before the chemical change as there are afterward.

Baking causes chemical changes. A cake is made of flour, sugar, milk, and eggs. But eating these things without mixing and baking them is not the same as eating cake! When you bake the mixture, a chemical change takes place. The atoms of the mixture re-form to create atoms of a new substance, cake.

Chemical changes even take place inside your body. In fact, you could not live without them. Chemical changes turn the food you eat into substances your body can use.

A. Fill in the missing words.

1. A chemical change happens whenever there is a change in a substance's _____molecules_____. (molecules, shape)

2. Chemical changes always make new _____substances_____. (atoms, substances)

3. Burning wood is a _____chemical_____ change. (physical, chemical)

4. When iron atoms join with oxygen atoms, they form _____rust_____. (rust, flames)

5. _____Matter_____ is never lost in a chemical change. (Rust, Matter)

B. Write the letter for the correct answer.

1. A ___c___ change happens whenever there is a change in a substance's molecules.
   (a) physical   (b) temperature   (c) chemical

2. In a chemical change, ___a___ causes the atoms to break free of their molecules and form different molecules.
   (a) energy   (b) water   (c) smoke

3. When wood burns, it is changed into ashes and ___b___.
   (a) water   (b) smoke   (c) oxygen

4. There are always exactly the same number of ___c___ before a chemical change as there are afterward.
   (a) formulas   (b) compounds   (c) atoms

C. Answer the questions.

1. Why is rusting iron a chemical change? _____Iron atoms join with oxygen atoms to form molecules of rust._____

2. How do the chemical changes that take place inside your body help you? _____They turn the food you eat into substances your body can use._____

27

Chemical Reactions

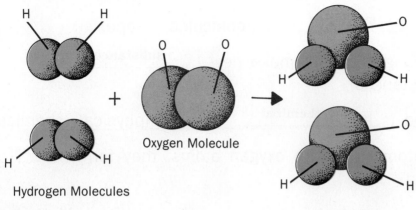

Hydrogen Molecules

Oxygen Molecule

Water Molecules

Chemical changes are called **chemical reactions.** Scientists have a special way of showing what happens in a chemical reaction. You have learned that every element has a symbol, such as O for oxygen and H for hydrogen. You also know that scientists use these symbols in formulas that describe molecules. H_2O is the formula that describes a water molecule.

In chemical reactions, molecules are changed. Scientists use formulas in equations to show these changes. Instead of an equal sign, chemical equations use an arrow. Because matter is never lost in a chemical reaction, the number of atoms is the same on both sides of the arrow.

This equation shows how hydrogen and oxygen combine to form water.

$$2H_2 + O_2 \rightarrow 2H_2O$$

A drawing of this equation is at the top of the page. On the left side of the equation are two molecules of hydrogen and one molecule of oxygen. Energy causes these molecules to break apart. Then the atoms form new molecules. You can see the new molecules on the right side of the equation. The new molecules are water molecules. You can see that there is the same number of each kind of atom on each side of the equation. No matter has been lost.

A. **Write the letter for the correct answer.**

1. H is the symbol for _____a_____ .
   (a) hydrogen   (b) oxygen   (c) an atom

2. O is the symbol for _____a_____ .
   (a) oxygen   (b) hydrogen   (c) an atom

3. Formulas describe _____b_____ .
   (a) atoms   (b) molecules   (c) chemical reactions

4. Scientists use formulas in _____c_____ to show chemical changes.
   (a) charts   (b) test tubes   (c) equations

5. Instead of an equal sign, chemical equations use _____b_____ .
   (a) a circle   (b) an arrow   (c) a square

B. **Underline the correct words.**

1. Chemical changes are called chemical (<u>reactions</u>, events).

2. Every element has a (color, <u>symbol</u>).

3. H_2O is the formula for (<u>water</u>, wood).

4. In a chemical equation, the number of (substances, <u>atoms</u>) is the same on both sides of the arrow.

5. (<u>Energy</u>, Water) causes molecules to break apart.

6. Formulas describe (equations, <u>molecules</u>).

C. **Answer the questions.**

1. In a chemical equation, why is the number of atoms the same on both sides of the arrow? _____The number of atoms is the_____
   _____same because matter is never lost in a chemical_____
   _____reaction._____

2. What kind of molecule does the formula H_2O describe? _____H_2O_____
   _____is a formula that describes a water molecule._____

Acids, Bases, and Salts

Citrus fruits have citric acid in them.

Many detergents have bases in them.

Table salt is one kind of neutral salt.

Three kinds of compounds are **acids, bases,** or **salts.** Acids and bases are chemical <u>opposites</u>. A salt is produced by the chemical reaction of an acid with a base. Different **ions** are produced when an acid or a base breaks up in water. Many bases and acids react together to make new products.

<u>Litmus paper</u> is a special kind of paper. Scientists use litmus paper to tell whether something is an acid or a base. Acids turn blue litmus paper red. Bases turn red litmus paper blue.

Acids taste sour. Some of them can burn your skin. Some are weak. Weak acids are found in many kinds of food. Other acids are strong. Some strong acids can dissolve metal! Bases taste bitter. They feel soapy and slippery. Some bases can burn your skin. Bases that can be dissolved in water are called **alkalis.**

Acids and alkalis neutralize each other. This means that the negative electric charge of the alkali balances the positive electric charge of the acid. When a certain amount of acid and alkali is mixed together, a chemical change takes place. The acid and alkali turn into a neutral salt and water. Neutral salts cannot burn the skin like acids and bases. Table salt is one kind of neutral salt.

Acids and bases have many uses. Acids in your stomach help you digest food. Acids are used in making many things, such as paper. Bases are often used in cleansers. Both acids and bases are used in making some kinds of cloth.

A. Use the words below to complete the sentences.

alkalis	neutral	reaction
bases	neutralize	salts

1. Three kinds of compounds are acids, bases, or ____salts____.

2. Acids are the chemical opposite of ____bases____.

3. A salt is produced by the ____reaction____ of an acid with a base.

4. Bases that can be dissolved in water are called ____alkalis____.

5. Acids and alkalis ____neutralize____ each other.

6. Table salt is one kind of ____neutral____ salt.

B. Answer <u>True</u> or <u>False</u>.

1. Acids taste sour. ____True____

2. Acids cannot burn your skin. ____False____

3. Weak acids are found in many kinds of food. ____True____

4. Bases taste sweet. ____False____

5. Acids and bases do not react together. ____False____

6. Acids and alkalis neutralize each other. ____True____

7. There are acids in your stomach that help you digest food.
____True____

8. Bases are often used in cleansers. ____True____

C. Draw lines to complete the sentences.

1. Bases — turn blue litmus paper red.

2. Acids — feel soapy and slippery.

3. Alkalis — cannot burn your skin.

4. Salts — are bases that can be dissolved in water.

Chemicals Are Everywhere!

All these things have chemicals in them.

Chemicals are an important part of the world around you. You use hundreds of chemicals every day. They can help you to stay healthy.

There are chemicals in the food you eat. Protein is a chemical found in meat, fish, cheese, eggs, and beans. Protein helps you grow and build a strong body. Carbohydrates, the chemicals found in bread, cereal, pasta, and vegetables, give you energy. Vitamins and minerals are chemicals that help your body to use food. Sometimes chemicals are added to food to keep it fresh or give it a different taste.

Chemicals help you keep clean and healthy. They help you clean your home, too. Soap, shampoo, toothpaste, and detergents are all made of chemicals. Medicine is made of chemicals, too. The chemicals in medicine help your body fight disease.

Answer True or False.

1. There are not any chemicals in the food you eat. ___False___

2. Protein is a chemical found in meat, fish, cheese, eggs, and beans. ___True___

3. Carbohydrates are chemicals that give you energy. ___True___

4. Medicine is not made of chemicals. ___False___

Part A

Use the words below to complete the sentences.

chemical	molecule	reactions
compound	neutralize	solution
mixtures	physical	temperature

1. A _____molecule_____ is a group of atoms.

2. A _____compound_____ is a substance that is made from molecules of more than one element.

3. Most of the things you see in everyday life are _____mixtures_____ .

4. A mixture that does not look like a mixture and is not easy to separate back into its parts is called a _____solution_____ .

5. A _____physical_____ change is any change in matter that does not change the matter's molecules.

6. The state that matter is in depends mostly on its _____temperature_____ .

7. A _____chemical_____ change happens whenever there is a change in a substance's molecules.

8. Chemical changes are called chemical _____reactions_____ .

9. Acids and alkalis _____neutralize_____ each other.

Part B

Read each sentence. Write **True** if the sentence is true. Write **False** if the sentence is false.

1. Every molecule in a compound is exactly the same. ___True___

2. Chemical changes always make new substances. ___True___

3. Acids taste bitter and feel soapy and slippery. ___False___

4. There are chemicals in the food you eat. ___True___

EXPLORE & DISCOVER

Test for a Solution

You Need

- colored chalk
- scissors
- small bowl
- metal or wooden spoon
- water
- tall plastic or paper cup
- filter paper or coffee filter

1. Find out if chalk and water make a mixture or a solution. Hold a piece of chalk over a small bowl and cut off a few small bits.

2. Use the back of the spoon to grind the chalk into a powder.

3. Add a small amount of water (about $\frac{1}{4}$ cup) and stir until the chalk and water are well mixed.

4. Fold the filter paper over the top of the cup. Then pour the chalk and water through the filter.

5. If you have a **solution,** all the chalk and water will go through the filter. If you have a **mixture,** the chalk will be filtered out and trapped by the filter paper.

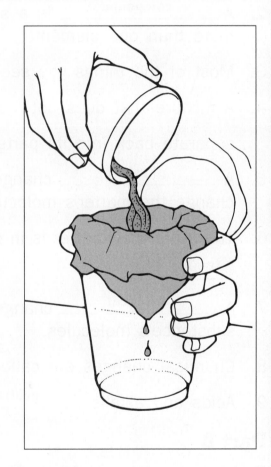

Write the Answer

Tell what happened. Do chalk and water make a solution or a mixture?

The water went through the filter, but the chalk

(or most of the chalk) was trapped by the filter paper.

Chalk and water make a mixture, not a solution.

Fill in the circle in front of the word or phrase that best completes each sentence. The first one is done for you.

1. A molecule is a group of
   ● atoms.
   ⓑ elements.
   ⓒ mixtures.

2. Bases that can be dissolved in water are called
   ⓐ alkalis.
   ⓑ acids.
   ⓒ metalloids.

3. A mixture can always be separated back into
   ⓐ water and salt.
   ⓑ the substances from which it was made.
   ⓒ hydrogen and oxygen.

4. Chemical changes always make
   ⓐ water.
   ⓑ new substances.
   ⓒ acids.

5. Every molecule in a compound is
   ⓐ different.
   ⓑ soft.
   ⓒ exactly the same.

6. A physical change is any change in matter that does not change the matter's
   ⓐ state.
   ⓑ shape.
   ⓒ molecules.

Fill in the missing words.

7. When ice is heated it turns into a _____liquid_____. (liquid, new substance)

8. The chemical protein is found in _____meat_____. (pasta, meat)

9. Acids are the chemical opposite of _____bases_____. (water, bases)

Write the answer on the lines.

10. What kind of change occurs when there is a change in a substance's molecules?

   A chemical change occurs
   _____
   whenever there is a change in a substance's molecules.

UNIT 3
Nature's Energies

What Is Energy?

Jumping and running take energy.

A car uses energy to move.

Imagine you have been swimming for a long time. You are tired. Some friends ask you to play volleyball. You say that you do not have the energy. What exactly do you mean? What is energy?

Energy is the ability to do work. Moving things is a type of work. When you hit a volleyball, you move it. When you jump and run, you move yourself. Playing volleyball, jumping, and running all take energy.

There are several kinds of energy. One kind of energy is **mechanical energy.** Whenever anything moves, it is using mechanical energy. A second kind of energy is **heat energy.** Heat energy passes heat from one object to another. A third kind of energy is **electric energy.** Electric energy makes light bulbs light up and radios play. A fourth kind of energy is **chemical energy.** Gasoline has chemical energy. When gasoline is burned in a car's engine, the chemical energy is changed to mechanical energy. The mechanical energy moves the car.

Energy is not matter, because it does not have mass or take up space. You cannot see energy, but you can see what energy does. Each kind of energy can change into other kinds of energy. In this unit you will learn about different kinds of energy.

Use the words below to complete the sentences.

chemical	Energy	matter
Electric	Heat	mechanical

1. _____Energy_____ is the ability to do work.

2. Whenever anything moves, it is using _____mechanical_____ energy.

3. _____Heat_____ energy passes heat from one object to another.

4. _____Electric_____ energy makes light bulbs light up and radios play.

5. Gasoline has _____chemical_____ energy.

6. Energy is not _____matter_____ .

B. **Answer True or False.**

1. There is only one kind of energy. _____False_____

2. When you jump and run, you do work. _____True_____

3. Gasoline has heat energy. _____False_____

4. Each kind of energy can change into other kinds of energy.

   _____True_____

5. It does not take energy to hit a volleyball. _____False_____

6. Heat energy passes heat from one object to another. _____True_____

7. Energy has mass and takes up space. _____False_____

C. **Answer the questions.**

1. What are four kinds of energy? _____Four kinds of energy are_____
   _____mechanical energy, heat energy, electric energy, and_____
   _____chemical energy._____

2. What is energy? _____Energy is the ability to do_____
   _____work._____

Energy from the Sun

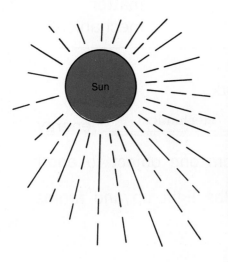

Carbon Dioxide from the Air

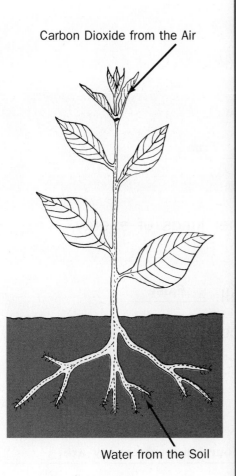

Water from the Soil

Plants need the energy of the sun to make food from water and carbon dioxide.

All the energy in the world comes from the sun. The sun's energy is called **solar energy.** On Earth, solar energy is changed to other kinds of energy. Nothing on Earth could live without energy from the sun.

Plants could not live without solar energy. Plants make their own food. They use energy from the sun to make their food. They make food out of water from the soil and the gas in air called carbon dioxide. People eat the food that plants make. Apples, potatoes, lettuce, celery, and beans are all plant foods that people eat. Without solar energy, people would not have any plants to eat.

Some animals also eat plants. Animals eat other animals that eat plants. Without plants, animals could not live. There would be no animals for people to eat. You would not have chicken or hamburgers or fish to eat. You would not have the things that animals produce, such as milk, eggs, or wool, either.

People are warmed by the heat of the sun. When it is cold, people use fuels such as coal and oil to heat their homes. These fuels were made by solar energy. Coal and oil were formed from plants and animals that lived millions of years ago. When the plants and animals died, their bodies became part of Earth. The energy from these dead plants and animals became the chemical energy in coal and oil. When coal and oil are burned, the stored chemical energy becomes heat energy.

A. **Write the letter for the correct answer.**

1. All energy comes from ____c____ .
   (a) plants   (b) animals   (c) the sun

2. Plants could not live without ____b____ energy.
   (a) fuel   (b) solar   (c) mechanical

3. Plants make their own ____b____ .
   (a) energy   (b) food   (c) water

4. The energy from dead plants and animals became the ____a____ energy in coal and oil.
   (a) chemical   (b) mechanical   (c) electric

5. When fuels are burned, chemical energy becomes ____c____ energy.
   (a) mechanical   (b) electric   (c) heat

B. **Name the three things that plants use to make their own food. Choose from the words below.**

carbon dioxide	energy from the sun
coal	water from the soil

1. _____ carbon dioxide _____

2. _____ energy from the sun _____

3. _____ water from the soil _____

C. **Answer True or False.**

1. All energy comes from the sun. ____True____

2. Without solar energy, people would not have any plants to eat.
   ____True____

3. Energy from the sun is called food energy. ____False____

4. On Earth, solar energy is changed into other kinds of energy.
   ____True____

5. Coal and oil were formed from carbon dioxide and water. ____False____

Heat Energy

Hot soup heats a metal spoon by conduction.

Convection currents heat water.

The sun heats by radiation.

Heat energy is energy passed as heat from one object to another. Heat always passes from a hotter object to a cooler object. If you hold an ice cube in your hand, it will start to melt. Heat energy passes from your hand to the ice cube. The heat energy makes the molecules in the ice move faster. The ice begins to melt, or become a liquid.

Heat energy can be passed in three ways. One way is by **conduction.** Heat passes through solids by conduction. When one object passes heat to another by conduction, the heat keeps flowing until both objects are equally hot.

Have you ever eaten hot soup with a metal spoon? After a while, the spoon gets hot. The hot soup causes the molecules in the spoon to move faster. The heat travels from the soup up the spoon to your hand.

Convection is the way heat passes through liquids and gases. Molecules in liquids and gases move apart when they are heated. This happens during convection. When you heat water on the stove, the bottom layer of water is heated first. The molecules in this layer of water move farther apart. This layer floats to the top, and the cooler, heavier water on top falls to the bottom. These movements are called **convection currents.** In winter, convection heats the air in your house.

The third way of passing heat energy is by **radiation.** Radiation moves in waves. Solar heat comes in radiation waves. Microwave ovens heat food by radiation.

A. Fill in the missing words.

1. Heat energy is energy passed as ____heat____ from one object to another. (heat, wind)

2. In winter, ____convection____ heats the air in your house. (convection, radiation)

3. Heat energy can be passed in ___three___ ways. (three, ten)

4. Heat passes through solids by ____conduction____. (convection, conduction)

B. Answer True or False.

1. Heat passes from a cooler object to a hotter object. ___False___

2. In convection, heat is passed by movements called convection currents. ___True___

3. Solar heat comes in radiation waves. ___True___

4. Molecules in liquids and gases move apart when they are heated. ___True___

C. Use the words below to complete the sentences. You will use each word twice.

conduction	convection	radiation

1. Microwave ovens heat food by ____radiation____.

2. When one object passes heat to another by ____conduction____, the heat keeps flowing until both objects are equally hot.

3. When you heat water on the stove, heat is passed by ____convection____ currents.

4. A spoon in hot soup is heated by ____conduction____.

5. The passing of heat energy in waves is ____radiation____.

6. In winter, the air in your house is heated by ____convection____.

Energy from Wind

Sailboats are powered by wind energy.

Windmills use wind energy to make electricity.

Wind is caused by heat from the sun. The sun heats air by convection. The convection currents that move through heated water also move through heated air. The moving air is called wind.

The sun warms the surface of Earth. Some parts of Earth's surface, such as roads and beaches, absorb, or take in, more heat than others. The air over these areas becomes warmer than the air around them. This warm air rises, and the cool air around it moves in to take its place. This convection current happens anywhere that air becomes heated. Sometimes the air moves slowly. You cannot feel the wind at all. Sometimes it moves fast.

Wind is a source of mechanical energy. Any matter that is moving is using mechanical energy. The wind can move things. A very strong wind can push over trees and buildings.

One of the ways people use energy from wind is to power sailboats. As the wind pushes against the sails, it moves the boat across the water. Windmills are another way people use energy from wind. A windmill has flat blades on a wheel. Wind pushes the blades and makes the wheel turn. The energy of the turning wheel can be used to pump water from a well. It can also be used to make electricity. People have been using windmills for more than a thousand years.

A. Fill in the missing words.

1. Wind is caused by heat from the ____sun____ . (sun, oceans)

2. A ____convection____ current happens anywhere that air becomes heated. (conduction, convection)

3. Some parts of Earth's surface, such as ____beaches____ , absorb more heat than others. (beaches, mountains)

4. Warm air rises, and ____cool____ air around it moves in to take its place. (fast, cool)

5. ____Moving____ air is wind. (Hot, Moving)

6. Wind is a source of ____mechanical____ energy. (mechanical, heat)

7. ____Windmills____ are a way people use energy from wind. (Radios, Windmills)

8. People have been using windmills for ____more than a thousand____ years. (more than a thousand, ten)

B. Answer True or False.

1. Moving air is called wind. ____True____

2. The sun heats air by convection. ____True____

3. Cool air rises, and the warm air around it moves in to take its place. ____False____

4. Sailboats use electrical energy. ____False____

5. Air always moves slowly. ____False____

6. Wind is a source of mechanical energy. ____True____

C. Answer the questions.

1. What causes wind? ____Wind is caused by heat from the sun.____

2. Name two ways people use wind energy. ____People use wind energy for sailboats and windmills.____

Energy from Water

A Waterwheel

Hoover Dam

Moving water can push on objects and move them. Remember that any matter that is moving is using mechanical energy. So water is a source of mechanical energy. Mechanical energy from water is used in many ways.

A long time ago, people learned to use energy from water for waterwheels. Waterwheels are built on streams. A waterwheel is a large wheel with blades on it. As water pushes on the blades, the wheel turns. Even today, energy from waterwheels is used to grind grain and cut logs.

When water falls from a high place to a lower place, it carries a lot of energy. Dams are built on rivers and lakes to make use of this energy. Dams hold back a great amount of water. This water is sent through pipes to **water turbines** hundreds of feet below. A turbine is like a waterwheel, but it turns much faster. The falling water turns the turbines. The water energy that the turbines collect is then used to run a **generator.** The generator makes electricity.

A lot of electricity can be made by dams. The Hoover Dam, on the border between Arizona and Nevada, is one of the highest dams in the world. It sends electricity to Arizona, California, and Nevada.

Water is a good source of energy. It does not pollute the air. It will never run out. But water power plants can be built only near a waterfall or dam. Also, dams cost a great deal of money to build. All energy cannot come from water.

A. **Use the words below to complete the sentences.**

dam	generator	water
electricity	mechanical	waterwheels
energy	turbine	wind

1. Any matter that is moving is using _____mechanical_____ energy.

2. Mechanical energy from _____water_____ uses the push of water as a source of power.

3. A long time ago, people learned to use energy from water for _____waterwheels_____.

4. When water falls from a high place to a lower place, it carries a lot of _____energy_____.

5. A _____turbine_____ is like a waterwheel.

6. Energy from the push of water that a turbine collects is used to run a _____generator_____.

7. A generator makes _____electricity_____.

8. Water power plants can be built only near a waterfall or a _____dam_____.

B. **The sentences below tell how falling water makes electricity. Number the sentences in the correct order. The first one is done for you.**

___3___ Water turns the turbines.

___1___ The dam holds back water.

___4___ The turbines collect energy to run a generator.

___5___ The generator makes electricity.

___2___ Water is sent through pipes to water turbines hundreds of feet below.

45

Energy from Steam

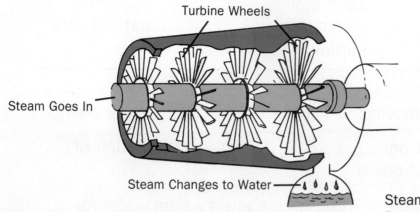

Turbine Wheels

Steam Goes In

Steam Changes to Water

Steam Turbine Operating a Ship's Propeller

When water boils, it turns into a gas. This gas is called **steam.** Steam can push on objects and move them. Any matter that is moving is using mechanical energy. Steam is a source of mechanical energy. The push of steam provides energy that can be used in many important ways.

Steam is made in a boiler. A boiler has a large tank and a furnace. The tank holds water, and the furnace burns fuel to heat the water. Coal, oil, and wood are three kinds of fuel used to produce steam. When the fuel burns, the chemical energy stored in it changes into heat energy. The heat energy heats the water in the boiler and changes it into steam.

You have learned that wind and water can turn wheels with blades. Steam can also turn wheels with blades. This kind of wheel is called a **steam turbine.** The energy from steam turbines can be used in many ways.

Many large ships get their energy from steam engines. The steam turbines on these ships turn the ships' propellers. Propellers make the ships move through the water.

Steam turbines are also used to make electricity. Energy from the turbines is used to run generators, which make electricity. Many large electric power plants have steam turbines.

A. Write the letter for the correct answer.

1. When water boils, it turns into a gas called ___b___ .
   (a) heat   (b) steam   (c) electricity

2. Steam is made in a ___a___ .
   (a) boiler   (b) waterwheel   (c) steam turbine

3. When fuel burns, the chemical energy stored in it changes into ___c___ energy.
   (a) electric   (b) mechanical   (c) heat

4. The energy from steam ___a___ can be used in many ways.
   (a) turbines   (b) generators   (c) propellers

5. Steam turbines on a ship turn the ship's ___b___ .
   (a) generators   (b) propellers   (c) furnaces

6. Steam turbines are also used to make ___c___ .
   (a) fuel   (b) water   (c) electricity

B. Answer True or False.

1. Many large ships get their energy from steam engines. ___True___

2. Many large electric power plants have steam turbines. ___True___

3. Steam is a source of mechanical energy. ___True___

4. Propellers make ships move through the water. ___True___

5. Steam is a liquid. ___False___

6. A furnace uses electricity to heat water. ___False___

7. Energy from steam turbines can be used to run electric generators.
   ___True___

C. Answer the questions.

1. What are the two parts of a boiler? ___The two parts of a boiler are the tank and the furnace.___

2. What are three kinds of fuel used to produce steam? ___Three kinds of fuel used to produce steam are coal, oil, and wood.___

Nuclear Energy

Nuclear Power Plant

There is energy stored in the nucleus of an atom. You have learned that the nucleus is the center of an atom. The protons and neutrons in the nucleus are held together by a very strong force. Scientists can split the nuclei of some atoms. They fire neutrons at the nuclei at high speeds. When the nuclei split, they give off a large amount of energy. This energy is called **nuclear energy.**

Nuclear energy is produced in **nuclear reactors.** Nuclear reactors have very thick walls. Inside, heat energy from the splitting atoms is used to heat water and make steam. The steam is then used to make electricity.

Nuclear energy does not pollute the air. You might think that nuclear energy is the perfect source of energy. But the atoms that scientists split to make electricity are atoms of the element uranium. There is not much uranium in the world. One day it will all be gone. Also, nuclear energy can be dangerous. Atomic bombs use the energy from splitting atoms.

When an atom splits, it gives off radiation. Radiation can make people very sick. Also, the splitting of atoms leaves behind dangerous wastes. Many people think that nuclear energy is too dangerous to use. Others think that it can be controlled. Today, nuclear energy provides only a small part of the world's energy.

A. Answer True or False.

1. The nucleus is the center of an atom. ___True___

2. The protons and neutrons in the nucleus are held together by a very weak force. ___False___

3. The energy given off by the splitting of atomic nuclei is called nuclear energy. ___True___

4. Nuclear energy is produced in windmills. ___False___

5. When an atom splits, it gives off radiation. ___True___

6. Today, nuclear energy provides only a small part of the world's energy. ___True___

B. Draw lines to complete the sentences.

1. Nuclear energy ——————— is produced in nuclear reactors.

2. Scientists — can make people very sick.

3. Radiation — are held together by a strong force.

4. Protons and neutrons — can split the nuclei of some atoms.

C. Fill in the missing words.

1. There is energy stored in the ___nucleus___ of an atom. (nucleus, walls)

2. Scientists split nuclei by firing neutrons at them at ___high___ speeds. (low, high)

3. When the nuclei split, they give off a ___large___ amount of energy. (small, large)

4. Nuclear energy ___does not___ pollute the air. (does not, does)

5. When an atom splits, it gives off ___radiation___. (steam, radiation)

6. Radiation can make people very ___sick___. (sick, healthy)

Our Energy Needs

Burning fuels give off smoke.

Fuels such as gasoline will not last forever.

Americans use much more energy than people in other countries. Most Americans have cars, TVs, radios, and many other things that use energy. Many Americans also waste energy. They leave lights and radios on when they are not using them. It is important not to waste energy.

Most of the energy Americans use is from fuels, such as coal, oil, and gasoline. When these fuels are burned, they give off smoke. The smoke pollutes the air. There is another problem with these fuels. They will not last forever.

Today people are trying to find better ways to use energy from wind, water, and the sun. These sources of energy are clean. They will last forever. People are also trying to conserve energy. If everyone works to find better sources of energy and use less of it, there will be plenty of energy for the future.

Underline the correct words.

1. Americans use much more (energy, smoke) than people in other countries.

2. Most of the energy Americans use is from (waste, fuels), such as coal, oil, and gasoline.

3. Smoke (cleans, pollutes) the air.

4. People are trying to (conserve, burn) energy.

Part A

Write the letter for the correct answer.

1. Whenever anything moves, it is using ____a____ energy.
   (a) mechanical   (b) heat   (c) chemical

2. All the energy in the world comes from ____c____.
   (a) plants   (b) coal   (c) the sun

3. Heat energy always passes from a ____b____ object to a cooler object.
   (a) smaller   (b) hotter   (c) larger

4. ____a____ is caused by convection currents.
   (a) Wind   (b) Steam   (c) Heat

5. Dams are built on rivers and lakes to make use of ____c____ energy.
   (a) wind   (b) electric   (c) water

6. The energy given off when the nuclei of atoms split is ____c____.
   (a) solar energy   (b) electric energy   (c) nuclear energy

7. Today people are trying to find better ways to use energy from wind, water, and ____a____.
   (a) the sun   (b) the moon   (c) oil

Part B

Draw lines to complete the sentences.

1. Mechanical energy   is the energy that comes from the push of water.

2. Heat energy   changes into the other kinds of energy.

3. Water energy   is used by any matter that is moving.

4. Solar energy   is passed as heat from one object to another.

5. Wind energy   is given off when the nucleus of an atom splits.

6. Nuclear energy   comes from moving air.

Make a Water Wheel

You Need

- thread spool
- scissors
- straw or pencil
- large plastic pan
- milk carton
- tape
- pitcher of water

1. Make a water wheel. Use an empty thread spool for the wheel and pieces of a milk carton for the blades.

2. Cut four squares from the milk carton. The length of the squares should be a bit shorter than the length of your spool.

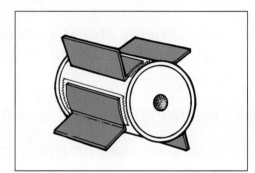

3. Fold each square in half and tape half of it onto your spool as shown in the top picture. The blades should be spaced evenly around the spool.

4. Stick a straw or a pencil through the spool. Then hold your water wheel over a pan and pour water on it as shown in the bottom picture. Or, hold the water wheel under a faucet.

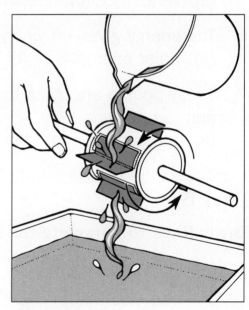

5. A windmill is like a water wheel that is powered by wind. Blow on your water wheel. How could the wind power be used?

Write the Answer

How does a water wheel work? How does a windmill work?

The energy of falling water turns the water wheel, and the energy

of moving air turns the windmill. The mechanical energy given to

these machines can be used to run other machinery connected to them.

Fill in the circle in front of the word or phrase that best completes each sentence. The first one is done for you.

1. When water boils, it turns into a gas called
   - (a) heat.
   - ● steam.
   - (c) energy.

2. Wind energy is a source of
   - (a) water energy.
   - (b) chemical energy.
   - (c) mechanical energy.

3. Many large electric power plants have
   - (a) steam turbines.
   - (b) windmills.
   - (c) propellers.

4. Moving water can push on objects and
   - (a) burn them.
   - (b) move them.
   - (c) heat them.

5. Coal and oil are kinds of
   - (a) fuel.
   - (b) plants.
   - (c) generators.

6. The energy given off when the nuclei of atoms split is
   - (a) heat energy.
   - (b) mechanical energy.
   - (c) nuclear energy.

Fill in the missing words.

7. Energy from the sun is called _____solar_____ energy. (heat, solar)

8. When an atom splits, it gives off _____radiation_____. (convection, radiation)

9. Energy is the ability to _____do work_____. (smell, do work)

Write the answer on the lines.

10. What is the source of all the world's energy?

   _____All of the energy in the world_____

   _____comes from the sun._____

UNIT 4
Sound and Light

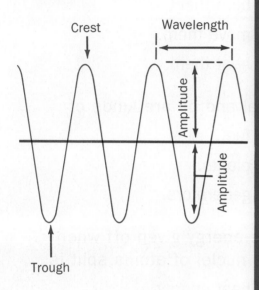

Crest

Wavelength

Amplitude

Amplitude

Trough

Sound Waves

Sounds are made by vibrating objects.

How Sound Travels

Have you ever thrown a rock into a lake or pond? Small waves move outward in a circle away from the place where the rock hit the water. Some kinds of energy move in waves like these. Sound is a kind of energy that moves in waves. Sound waves can move through all kinds of matter. You cannot see sound waves. But you know they are there because you can hear the sound.

All sounds are made by vibrating objects. To vibrate means to move quickly back and forth. When a vibrating object moves outward, it pushes the air molecules close together. Then they spread out again and push the molecules next to them. This movement of molecules is a sound wave. Sound waves, like waves in a pond, move outward in circles from their source.

Sound waves move more quickly through dense matter. The molecules of dense matter are close together. Sound travels faster through water than through air. This is because the molecules in water are much closer than the molecules in air.

Scientists use special words to describe waves. The highest part of a wave is called the **crest.** The lowest part of a wave is the **trough.** One half the distance between a wave's crest and its trough is the wave's **amplitude.** The **wavelength** of a sound is the distance between the crests of two of its waves. The number of waves that move past one spot in a second is the sound's **frequency.**

A. **Underline the correct words.**

1. Sound is a kind of energy that moves in (<u>waves</u>, space).

2. Sound waves (cannot, <u>can</u>) move through all kinds of matter.

3. All sounds are made by (still, <u>vibrating</u>) objects.

4. Sound waves, like waves in a pond, move (inward, <u>outward</u>) in circles from their source.

5. Sound waves move more quickly through (<u>dense</u>, light) matter.

6. The lowest part of a wave is the (crest, <u>trough</u>).

B. **Draw lines to match the parts of waves with their descriptions.**

1. crest — half the distance between a wave's crest and its trough

2. trough — the highest part of a wave

3. amplitude — number of waves that move past one spot in a second

4. wavelength — the lowest part of a wave

5. frequency — the distance between two crests

C. **Answer <u>True</u> or <u>False</u>.**

1. Energy does not move in waves. ___False___

2. Sound waves cannot move through matter. ___False___

3. You cannot see sound waves. ___True___

4. All sounds are made by vibrating objects. ___True___

5. Sound waves move outward in circles from the person hearing the sound. ___False___

6. Sound waves move more quickly through dense matter. ___True___

7. The molecules of dense matter are far apart. ___False___

8. The wavelength of a sound is the distance between the crests of two of its waves. ___True___

55

Pitch and Loudness

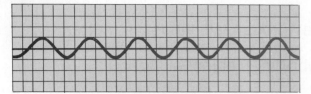

High-Pitched Soft Sound

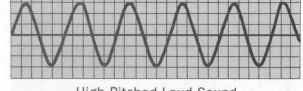

High-Pitched Loud Sound

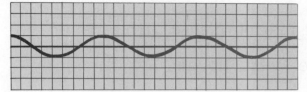

Low-Pitched Soft Sound

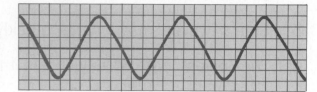

Low-Pitched Loud Sound

You have learned that all sounds are waves that move through the air. But not all sounds are alike. Some sounds, such as a bird singing, are high sounds. Other sounds, such as a frog croaking, are low sounds. Some sounds are so quiet you can barely hear them. Other sounds are very loud. What makes these sounds different?

The quality of being high or low is a sound's **pitch**. A sound's pitch is based on the frequency of its sound waves. You have learned that a sound's frequency is the number of waves that move past one spot in a second.

Waves with a high frequency have a high sound. These waves have short wavelengths. Waves with a low frequency have a low sound. These waves have long wavelengths.

A sound's loudness is different from its pitch. A high-pitched sound can be loud or soft. So can a low-pitched sound.

A sound's loudness is related to the amplitude of its sound waves. You have learned that a wave's amplitude is one half the distance between its crest and its trough. Soft sounds have a low amplitude. Loud sounds have a high amplitude. Look at the pictures on this page to see the difference between high, low, loud, and soft sound waves.

A. Use the words below to complete the sentences.

amplitude	Loud	pitch
frequency	loudness	Soft
high	low	

1. The quality of being high or low is a sound's _____pitch_____ .

2. A sound's pitch is based on the _____frequency_____ of its sound waves.

3. Waves with a high frequency have a _____high_____ sound.

4. Waves with a low frequency have a _____low_____ sound.

5. A sound's _____loudness_____ is different from its pitch.

6. A sound's loudness is related to the _____amplitude_____ of its sound waves.

7. _____Soft_____ sounds have a low amplitude.

8. _____Loud_____ sounds have a high amplitude.

B. Answer the questions.

1. What is a sound's pitch? _____The quality of being high or low_____ _____is a sound's pitch._____

2. What is a sound's frequency? _____A sound's frequency is the_____ _____number of waves that move past_____ _____one spot in one second._____

C. Answer True or False.

1. All sounds are waves that move through the air. _____True_____

2. Waves with a high frequency have a high sound. _____True_____

3. A sound's loudness is the same as its pitch. _____False_____

57

Music

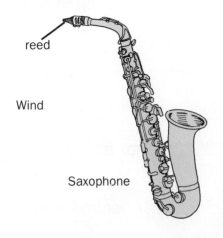

reed

Wind

Saxophone

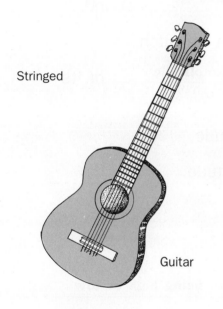

Stringed

Guitar

Percussion

Cymbals

The sounds that you hear can be divided into music and noise. What is the difference? Music is pleasant to listen to. Noise is not. Music is made of notes, or sounds with a certain pitch. These sounds have certain frequencies. Noise is made of sounds with different frequencies.

In music, each note lasts for a certain amount of time. The times that the different notes last make up a pattern. This pattern is the music's rhythm. Noise does not have rhythm.

When people sing, they make music with their voices. People also make music with instruments. The three main kinds are **wind, stringed,** and **percussion** instruments.

One kind of wind instrument, such as the saxophone, has a thin piece of wood called a reed that vibrates. The person playing the instrument blows into the mouthpiece, which has the reed attached to it. The vibrating reed makes the column of air inside the instrument vibrate.

The piano, the guitar, and the violin are stringed instruments. They make sounds by vibrating strings. The strings are hit by tiny hammers, plucked with the fingers, or moved with a bow. The vibrating strings cause the air around them to vibrate.

Percussion instruments, such as drums and cymbals, make sounds by being struck. When the instrument is struck, it vibrates and causes the air around it to vibrate. Most percussion instruments do not have any certain pitch. Instead, they mark the beat of the music.

A. Answer True or False.

1. Music is pleasant to listen to. __True__

2. Music is made of notes. __True__

3. Noise is made of sounds with the same frequencies. __False__

4. Noise is rhythm. __False__

5. When people sing, they make music with their voices. __True__

6. The piano is a wind instrument. __False__

7. Percussion instruments make sounds by vibrating strings. __False__

8. Stringed instruments make sounds by vibrating strings. __True__

9. Stringed instruments can make only noise. __False__

B. Choose the instrument that matches the type of instrument and write its name in the blank.

drums	guitar	saxophone

1. stringed instrument __guitar__

2. wind instrument __saxophone__

3. percussion instrument __drums__

C. Answer the question.

What are two reasons why music is different from noise? __Music is__ different from noise because music is pleasant to listen to, is made of notes, and has rhythm. Noise is not pleasant to listen to, is not made of notes, and does not have rhythm.

How You Hear

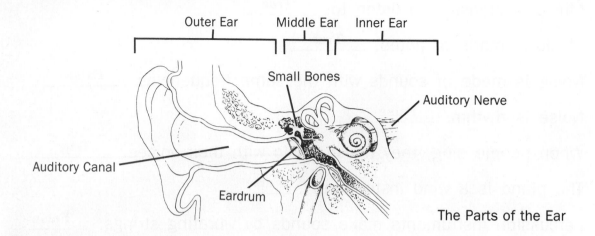

Outer Ear Middle Ear Inner Ear

Small Bones

Auditory Nerve

Auditory Canal

Eardrum

The Parts of the Ear

You hear many different sounds every day. You hear people talking. You hear music and the sounds of cars. You have learned that sound is caused by vibrations. Vibrations send sound waves through the air. But how do your ears turn these sound waves into the sounds you hear?

Your ear has three main parts. They are the outer ear, the middle ear, and the inner ear. The outside part of your ear catches sound waves moving through the air. Then the waves move down the **auditory canal.** You can see the opening of the auditory canal in the middle of your outer ear. The outside part of your ear and the auditory canal are both part of the outer ear.

Sound waves move down the auditory canal to the **eardrum.** The eardrum is a very thin **membrane** across the auditory canal. Sound waves make the eardrum vibrate. The vibrations from the eardrum are passed on to three small bones in the middle ear. The bones make the vibrations larger.

The inner ear is filled with liquid. The vibrations from the bones in the middle ear make the liquid move. The moving liquid bends tiny hairs in your inner ear. Your **auditory nerves** feel these hairs move. The auditory nerves turn these movements into signals and send them to the brain. These signals are the sounds you hear.

A. **The steps below describe how you hear. Number the steps in the correct order. The first one is done for you.**

_____3_____ The sound waves make the eardrum vibrate.

_____6_____ The moving liquid bends tiny hairs in your inner ear.

_____1_____ The outside part of your ear catches the sound waves moving through the air.

_____7_____ The auditory nerves turn the movements of the tiny hairs into signals and send them to the brain.

_____2_____ The sound waves move down the auditory canal.

_____5_____ The vibrations from the small bones in your middle ear make the liquid in your inner ear move.

_____4_____ Vibrations from the eardrum are passed to small bones.

B. **Underline the correct words.**

1. The outside part of your ear and the auditory canal are both part of the (outer, inner) ear.

2. The three small bones in the middle ear make the vibrations (smaller, larger).

3. The inner ear is filled with (liquid, air).

4. Sound waves move down the auditory canal to the (eardrum, outer ear).

5. The auditory nerves send signals to the (brain, eardrum).

6. Your (inner, middle) ear has three small bones.

7. Your ear has (six, three) main parts.

C. **Name the three parts of the ear.**

1. _____the outer ear_____

2. _____the middle ear_____

3. _____the inner ear_____

61

How You Talk

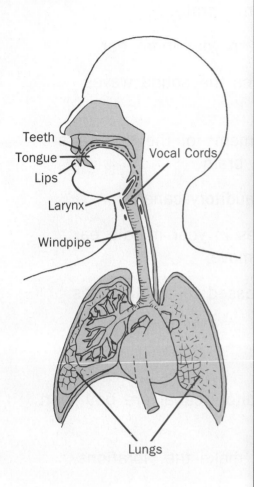

Teeth
Tongue
Lips
Larynx
Windpipe

Vocal Cords

Lungs

Parts of the Mouth and Throat

You have learned that all sounds are vibrations. When you speak, you send vibrations out into the air. Where do these vibrations come from?

Your voice begins in your **larynx,** or voice box. The voice box is the top part of your **windpipe.** Your **vocal cords** are small bands of <u>tissue</u> on either side of your voice box.

When you breathe, the vocal cords are relaxed. Your windpipe is completely open. When you talk, the muscles in your larynx pull on your vocal cords. The muscles pull the vocal cords over your windpipe. Only a narrow opening is left. The air coming up through your windpipe makes the vocal cords vibrate. These vibrations are sounds. When you talk, you use your mouth, tongue, teeth, and lips to shape these sounds into words.

Everyone talks the same way. But you can recognize the voices of people you know. This is because no two people have voices that sound exactly alike. Everyone's voice has its own pitch and its own sound.

The pitch of a person's voice depends on how large his or her voice box is. The larger a person's voice box is, the longer his or her vocal cords are. People with high voices have small voice boxes and short vocal cords. People with deep voices have large voice boxes and long vocal cords. People use their teeth, tongue, and lips differently when they talk. This is another reason why no two human voices sound exactly alike.

A. **Fill in the missing words.**

1. Your voice begins in your ___larynx___ . (larynx, mouth)

2. Your vocal cords are small bands of tissue on either side of your ___voice box___ . (voice box, mouth)

3. Air coming up through your windpipe makes your vocal cords ___vibrate___ . (relax, vibrate)

4. People with high voices have ___short___ vocal cords. (short, long)

5. People with low voices have ___long___ vocal cords. (short, long)

B. **Answer True or False.**

1. Your vocal cords are small bands of tissue on either side of your voice box. ___True___

2. When you breathe, your vocal cords are tight. ___False___

3. When you talk, your vocal cords are relaxed. ___False___

4. No two human voices sound exactly alike. ___True___

5. Everyone's voice has the same pitch and the same sound. ___False___

6. People with deep voices have large voice boxes and long vocal cords. ___True___

7. People use their teeth, tongue, and lips differently when they talk. ___True___

8. Your voice begins in your tongue. ___False___

C. **Use each word to write a sentence about how you talk.**

1. larynx _____ Sentences will vary. _____

_____

2. vocal cords _____

_____

How Light Travels

How Light Rays Bend

This girl can see her reflection in the mirror.

Light is a kind of energy. Light is given off in tiny particles called **photons.** Photons have no mass. They are not matter. Photons travel in waves. Most light waves have so many photons that the separate photons cannot be seen. They look like solid waves of light.

Sound waves are movements of the matter through which they travel. So sound waves can travel only through matter. But light waves are waves of photons. So light waves can travel through empty space.

Light travels very quickly. It goes through 186,225 miles of air in 1 second. Light travels much faster than sound. Sound goes only about one fifth of a mile in a second. Have you ever been in a thunderstorm? If you have, you may remember that you saw lightning a moment before you heard the thunder. The light from the lightning reached you more quickly than the sound did.

Light travels in straight lines called **rays.** When light rays hit a smooth, shiny surface such as a mirror, they bounce back. You see whatever is in front of the surface. This is called **reflection.**

Light rays cannot turn corners. But they can be bent by things in their path. When a light ray goes through a different substance, such as glass or water, it changes direction. Then the ray comes out on the other side and goes straight on. This is called **refraction.** Look at the picture of a straw in a glass of water. The straw is not really bent. The light rays that your eyes see are bent.

A. Use the words below to complete the sentences.

energy	matter	space
mass	photons	waves

Light is a kind of ___energy___. Light is given off in tiny particles called ___photons___. Photons have no ___mass___. They are not ___matter___. Photons travel in ___waves___.

B. Write the letter for the correct answer.

1. Sound waves can travel only through ___c___.
   (a) space   (b) water   (c) matter

2. Light travels much ___a___ than sound.
   (a) faster   (b) more slowly   (c) more loudly

3. Light travels in straight lines called ___b___.
   (a) particles   (b) rays   (c) photons

4. The bending of light rays by things in their path is called ___a___.
   (a) refraction   (b) reflection   (c) transmission

5. When light rays hit a smooth, shiny surface and bounce back, it is called ___c___.
   (a) transmission   (b) refraction   (c) reflection

6. Light is given off in tiny particles called ___b___.
   (a) electrons   (b) photons   (c) straws

C. Answer <u>True</u> or <u>False</u>.

1. Photons have mass. ___False___

2. Photons travel in waves. ___True___

3. Light goes only about one mile in a second. ___False___

4. Light is much faster than sound. ___True___

5. Light rays cannot turn corners. ___True___

Sources of Light

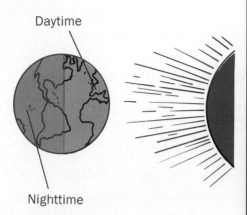

Daytime

Nighttime

How the Sun Lights Earth

Most of the light on Earth comes from the sun. The sun shines during the daytime. At night, the sun sets and it is dark. Why does the sun shine only during the day?

The sun is always shining. But because Earth **rotates,** or spins around, you see the sun's light only during the day. When the part of Earth where you are is facing the sun, sunlight falls on it. But as Earth spins, your part of Earth moves and faces away from the sun. Then it is night. Your nighttime is daytime for the people on the other side of Earth.

At night, some light comes from the moon. The moon does not really give off its own light. It just reflects light from the sun. So moonlight is very dim.

Most of the people in the world use electric light bulbs to see at night. The light from a light bulb comes from the **filament.** The filament is a small piece of tungsten wire. Electricity passes through the wire and makes it very hot. The hot wire gives off light.

Fill in the missing words.

1. Most of the light on Earth comes from the ___sun___. (sun, moon)

2. Because Earth ___rotates___, you see the sun's light only during the day. (is round, rotates)

3. Your nighttime is ___daytime___ for the people on the other side of Earth. (twilight, daytime)

4. The moon reflects light from ___the sun___. (the sun, Earth)

5. Moonlight is very ___dim___. (bright, dim)

Color

Every day, you see objects of many different colors. The objects do not really have colors. The colors come from light. An object has a certain color because of the way it <u>absorbs</u> light.

Sunlight is a mixture of light of all colors. Each color of light has a different wavelength. The photons of different colors have different energies. Red light has a long wavelength and low-energy photons. Violet light has a short wavelength and high-energy photons.

A red object, such as an apple, absorbs all colors of light except red. The red light is reflected. You see a red apple. White objects reflect all colors of light. Black objects absorb all colors of light.

The **spectrum** is all the colors of light. You can see the spectrum by using a **prism.** A prism is a piece of glass shaped like a triangle. When light passes through the prism, it is separated into all its different colors. The spectrum can also be seen in a rainbow. Rainbows happen when the sun shines after it has been raining. The drops of water in the sky act like tiny prisms to separate out the different colors of sunlight.

The different colors of light can be seen in a rainbow.

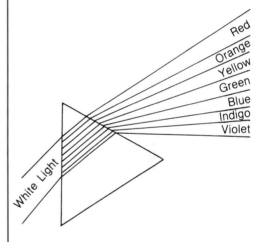

When light passes through a prism, it is separated into its different colors.

Answer <u>True</u> or <u>False</u>.

1. An object has a certain color because of the way it absorbs light.

   True

2. Sunlight is made of only one color of light. _False_

3. A red object reflects all colors of light except red. _False_

Lenses

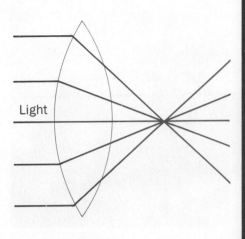

Convex Lens

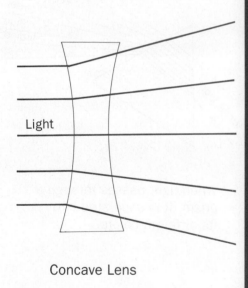

Concave Lens

You know that light can be refracted, or bent. **Lenses** are used for bending light. They can make objects look smaller or larger. They can make things that are far away look close. How do lenses work?

Lenses are made of glass or other materials that light can pass through. The two main kinds of lenses are **concave** lenses and **convex** lenses. A concave lens is thinner in the middle than it is at the edges. A concave lens bends light rays so that they spread apart. A convex lens is thicker in the middle than it is at the edges. A convex lens bends light rays so that they come together.

Lenses have many different uses. People who have trouble seeing wear eyeglasses or contact lenses. Eyeglasses are lenses worn in front of the eyes. Contact lenses are lenses worn on the eye. Contact lenses are made of plastic. Concave lenses help people who have trouble seeing objects in the distance. Convex lenses help people who have trouble seeing objects close to them.

Scientists use lenses in microscopes. The lenses in microscopes make very tiny objects look larger. Scientists use microscopes to study things that are normally too small to see. Scientists also use lenses in telescopes. Telescopes make faraway objects look as if they are closer. Scientists use telescopes to study stars and planets.

Lenses are used in cameras. They **focus** light on the film. Without lenses, there would not be photographs or movies!

A. Use the words below to complete the sentences.

closer	convex	light
concave	focus	microscopes

1. Lenses are used for bending _____*light*_____ .

2. A _____*concave*_____ lens is thinner in the middle than it is at the edges.

3. A _____*convex*_____ lens is thicker in the middle than it is at the edges.

4. The lenses in _____*microscopes*_____ make very tiny objects look larger.

5. Telescopes make objects that are very far away look _____*closer*_____ .

6. Lenses used in cameras _____*focus*_____ light on the film.

B. Answer True or False.

1. The main kinds of lenses are concave lenses and convex lenses.

   _____*True*_____

2. A concave lens bends light rays so that they come together.

   _____*False*_____

3. A convex lens bends light rays so that they come together.

   _____*True*_____

4. Lenses are used in cameras. _____*True*_____

5. Lenses are not used in telescopes. _____*False*_____

C. Answer the questions.

1. What do telescopes do? _____*Telescopes make objects that are*_____

   _____*very far away look closer.*_____

2. What do scientists use telescopes for? _____*Scientists use telescopes*_____

   _____*to study stars and planets.*_____

69

How You See

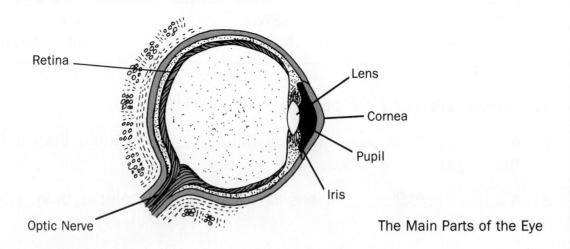

The Main Parts of the Eye

How do your eyes turn light into what you see? Your **eyeballs** are almost round. They have a thin covering called the **cornea.** The cornea helps to protect your eyes. The black circle in the middle of each of your eyes is the **pupil.** The pupil is a hole. Light goes through the pupil.

The colored part of your eye around the pupil is the **iris.** The iris changes the size of the pupil to let in the right amount of light. When the light is bright, the iris makes the pupil small. When the light is dim, it makes the pupil large.

Light enters the pupil and goes through the lens. The lens bends light rays so they hit the **retina** at the back of the eye. The retina is attached to the **optic nerve.** The optic nerve sends messages to your brain. Your brain sees these messages as pictures.

Draw lines to match each part of the eye with its description.

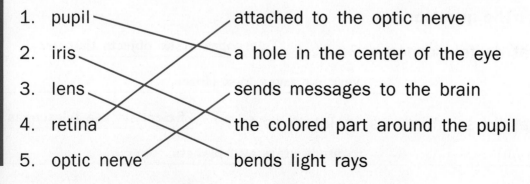

1. pupil   attached to the optic nerve

2. iris   a hole in the center of the eye

3. lens   sends messages to the brain

4. retina   the colored part around the pupil

5. optic nerve bends light rays

70

Part A

Underline the correct words.

1. Sound is a kind of energy that moves in (rays, <u>waves</u>).

2. All sounds are made by (<u>vibrating</u>, colored) objects.

3. The lowest part of a wave is called the (crest, <u>trough</u>).

4. The (<u>wavelength</u>, amplitude) of a sound is the distance between the crests of two of its waves.

5. A sound's pitch is based on the (amplitude, <u>frequency</u>) of its sound waves.

6. Your voice begins in your (<u>larynx</u>, eardrum).

7. Light is given off in tiny particles called (electrons, <u>photons</u>).

8. Light travels much (more slowly, <u>faster</u>) than sound.

9. Light travels in straight lines called (<u>rays</u>, refractions).

10. Because Earth (reflects, <u>rotates</u>), you see the sun's light only during the day.

Part B

Read each sentence. Write <u>True</u> if the sentence is true. Write <u>False</u> if the sentence is false.

1. Sound waves can move through all kinds of matter. ___True___

2. Sound waves move outward in squares from their source. ___False___

3. A sound's loudness is related to the amplitude of its sound waves.

    ___True___

4. Noise is made of notes. ___False___

5. The moon gives off its own light. ___False___

6. The light from a bulb comes from the filament. ___True___

7. An object that absorbs all colors of light is red. ___False___

Make Pepper Jump

You Need

- paper or plastic cup
- plastic wrap
- rubber band
- pepper
- radio or tape player
- metal baking pan
- ruler

1. Put plastic wrap over the top of the cup and secure it with a rubber band as shown in the picture. Make sure the plastic wrap is tight and smooth.

2. Shake a little pepper onto the center of the plastic wrap.

3. Put the cup on top of the speaker.

4. Turn the radio on and see what happens to the pepper. If nothing happens, turn the volume up and look again.

5. Hold the baking pan near the cup. Hit the pan with the ruler a few times and see what happens to the pepper.

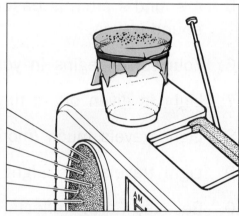

Write the Answer

In both cases, what makes the pepper jump?

The speaker and the pan both vibrate, causing the air molecules around

them to vibrate. When these vibrating air molecules hit the plastic wrap,

it vibrates, too, and makes the pepper jump.

Fill in the circle in front of the word or phrase that best completes each sentence. The first one is done for you.

1. Your voice begins in your
   - ● larynx.
   - ⓑ brain.
   - ⓒ auditory canal.

2. When light rays hit a smooth, shiny surface and bounce back, it is called
   - ⓐ concave.
   - ⓑ reflection.
   - ⓒ amplitude.

3. A concave lens bends light rays so that they
   - ⓐ change color.
   - ⓑ bounce back.
   - ⓒ spread apart.

4. Sound waves move more quickly through matter that is
   - ⓐ colored.
   - ⓑ dense.
   - ⓒ light.

5. Most percussion instruments do not have any certain
   - ⓐ pitch.
   - ⓑ beat.
   - ⓒ vibration.

6. The black circle in the middle of your eye is the
   - ⓐ retina.
   - ⓑ cornea.
   - ⓒ pupil.

Fill in the missing words.

7. The inner ear is filled with _____liquid_____. (air, liquid)

8. The auditory nerves send signals to the _____brain_____. (eardrum, brain)

9. Sound waves with a high frequency have a _____high_____ sound. (high, low)

Write the answer on the lines.

10. What is different about each color of light?

    Each color of light has a different wavelength.

UNIT 5
Magnetism and Electricity

Negative electrons moving from clouds to Earth caused this flash of lightning.

What Is Electricity?

Electricity is an important part of our lives. Electric lights help us see at night. Television gives us entertainment and news. Washers, refrigerators, and telephones make our lives easier.

Electricity is caused by matter that has an electric charge. You know that matter is made of atoms. Atoms are made of protons, neutrons, and electrons. The protons and neutrons are in the nucleus. Protons have a positive electric charge. Neutrons have no charge. So the nucleus has a positive charge. Electrons move around the nucleus. They have a negative charge. Things with opposite electric charges attract each other. So the electrons are attracted to the nucleus.

As long as an atom has an equal number of protons and electrons, the atom has no charge. But an atom can lose electrons. When you comb your hair, electrons may leave your hair and go to the comb. Because your hair has lost electrons, it now has a positive electric charge. The comb has gained electrons and it now has a negative electric charge. Your hair and the comb attract each other because they have opposite electric charges. This is an example of **static electricity.**

During a thunderstorm, particles in clouds rub together. This separates electrons from their atoms. The electrons build up in the clouds. If another cloud or something on Earth has a positive charge, the electrons move. The giant spark that results is called lightning.

A. **Answer True or False.**

1. Protons have a positive electric charge. __True__

2. Atoms are not made of any smaller particles. __False__

3. The electrons are in the nucleus. __False__

4. Things with opposite electric charges attract each other. __True__

5. An atom cannot lose electrons. __False__

6. When you comb your hair, you may cause static electricity.

   __True__

B. **Use the words below to complete the sentences.**

| atoms | matter | particles |
| Electricity | opposite | same |

1. __Electricity__ is an important part of our lives.

2. Electricity is caused by __matter__ that has an electric charge.

3. Matter is made of __atoms__ .

4. Things that have __opposite__ charges attract each other.

5. As long as an atom has the __same__ number of protons and electrons, it has no charge.

C. **Draw lines to match each particle with its description.**

1. proton — no electric charge

2. neutron — attracted to a positive charge

3. electron — attracted to a negative charge

D. **Name four things that use electricity.** __Answers may vary, but could include: electric lights, televisions, washers, refrigerators, and telephones.__

75

Electric Currents

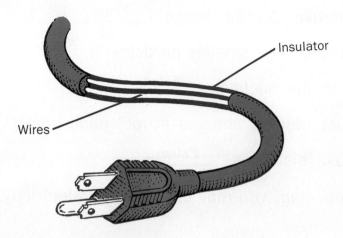

Inside an Electric Cord

You have learned that when electrons leave their atoms, matter becomes positively charged. Matter with extra electrons is negatively charged. If those electrons have a path to follow, they will flow to the area with positive charge. Electrically charged matter whose particles all move in the same direction is called **current electricity.**

Most of the electricity we use every day is current electricity. Current electricity is made by a generator. The generator gathers electrons. Then it pushes them all in the same direction. It forces electrons to move through a **conductor.**

A conductor is a kind of matter that electrons can move through easily. Metal wire is the conductor we use most to carry electricity. Matter that electrons cannot move through easily is an **insulator.** Rubber is a good insulator. Electric wires are often covered with rubber or plastic. This keeps the electrons from moving to any other conductor.

There are two kinds of current electricity. **Direct current** happens when the electrons flow in the same direction all the time. Batteries produce direct current electricity. **Alternating current** happens when the electron flow changes directions. The electric outlets in your house provide alternating current electricity.

A. Write the letter for the correct answer.

1. If extra electrons have a path to follow, they will flow to the area with ____c____ charge.
   (a) direct   (b) negative   (c) positive

2. Electrically charged matter whose particles all move in the same direction is called ____a____ electricity.
   (a) current   (b) static   (c) regular

3. Most of the electricity we use every day is ____c____ electricity.
   (a) static   (b) regular   (c) current

4. Current electricity is made by a ____a____ .
   (a) generator   (b) pump   (c) comb

5. A generator forces electrons to move through ____c____ .
   (a) an insulator   (b) a rope   (c) a conductor

6. Matter that electrons cannot move through easily is ____c____ .
   (a) a conductor   (b) a metal   (c) an insulator

7. ____a____ happens when the electron flow changes direction.
   (a) Alternating current   (b) Regular current   (c) Direct current

B. Answer True or False.

1. Rubber is the conductor we use for most of our needs. __False__

2. Batteries produce direct current electricity. __True__

3. The electric outlets in your house provide direct current electricity. __False__

4. Alternating current happens when the electrons flow in the same direction all the time. __False__

5. When electrons leave their atoms, matter becomes positively charged. __True__

6. Rubber that covers electric wires keeps electrons from moving to any other conductor. __True__

Electric Circuits and Volts

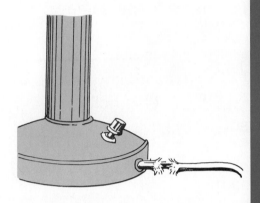

Broken insulation is dangerous.

The path taken by an electric current is called an electric **circuit.** Electric current flows from the source of the electricity through a wire. At the end of the wire is something that uses electricity. It may be a bulb in a lamp. The bulb is lighted by the electric current. But then the current must return to its source. The current has to make a complete circuit. That is why there are two wires in an electric cord. If the circuit has an opening, current will not flow.

Most electric circuits have a switch. When the switch is off, the circuit is open. The current's path is broken. The current cannot get back to its source. When the switch is on, there are no breaks in the path. It is a closed circuit. The current can complete its path.

Sometimes insulation that is wrapped around the wires wears out and breaks. Wires that should be kept separate may touch each other. Then electrons can move from wire to wire. They can take a shortcut in the path through the circuit. The shortcut is called a **short circuit.** Short circuits are dangerous. They can start fires.

Electric current is measured in **amperes.** The number of amperes tells how strong the current is. The amount of push a source of electricity gives the electricity is measured in **volts.** The number of volts tells how easily the current can move through the circuit. Some electrical energy always changes to heat energy. So a source must have enough extra volts to replace the lost electricity.

A. Underline the correct words.

1. The amount of push a source of electricity gives the electricity is measured in (<u>volts</u>, circuits).

2. Short circuits can (increase the number of volts, <u>start fires</u>).

3. When a lamp switch is (<u>on</u>, off), there are no breaks in the path.

4. Electric current is measured in (volts, <u>amperes</u>).

5. The path taken by an electric current is called an electric (source, <u>circuit</u>).

6. When a lamp switch is off, the current's path is (<u>broken</u>, not broken).

B. Use the words below to complete the sentences.

amperes	current	source
circuit	open	volts
closed	short circuit	

1. The path taken by an electric current is called an electric _____circuit_____ .

2. A current must return to its _____source_____ .

3. If the circuit has an opening, the _____current_____ will not flow.

4. When there are no breaks in the path, the circuit is ____closed____ .

5. When a switch is off, the circuit is _____open_____ .

6. When electrons can move from wire to wire, the shortcut is called a _____short circuit_____ .

7. The amount of push a source of electricity has is measured in _____volts_____ .

8. Electric current is measured in units called _____amperes_____ .

Fuses and Circuit Breakers

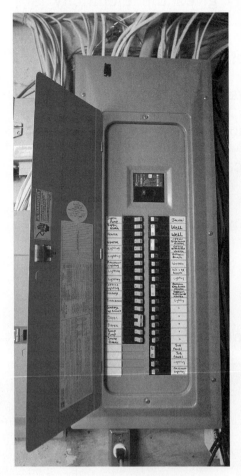

Circuit Breakers

You have learned that when electricity flows through a circuit, some electricity changes into heat. Sometimes too much current goes through a circuit. For instance, lightning can cause too much current in a circuit. When this happens, the device that is using the electricity can break. The wires of the circuit get very hot. The heat can start a fire.

To keep fires from starting, **fuses** are put in circuits. A fuse is like a little light bulb. It has a wire inside that melts easily. When the circuit has too much current, the wire heats up. The wire becomes so hot that it melts. The circuit is broken. The current cannot complete its path. The path is an open circuit. No more electricity can flow through it.

Every circuit usually has its own fuse. When a fuse breaks a circuit, a fresh fuse must be put in the place of the burned-out fuse. Otherwise the circuit will not work.

Circuit breakers are sometimes used instead of fuses. A circuit breaker has a switch that works like a fuse. If the electric current is too great, a switch opens and stops the current. When a circuit breaker breaks a circuit, it does not have to be replaced. The switch can be closed, and the circuit will work again.

Without fuses and circuit breakers, people would have no way of knowing if there were too much current in a circuit. There would be many more fires started by electricity. Fuses and circuit breakers help make electricity safe to use.

A. Answer True or False.

1. When electricity flows through a circuit, some electricity changes into heat. ____True____

2. If a circuit is open, the current can complete its path. ____False____

3. When a fuse breaks a circuit, a fresh fuse must be put in the place of the burned-out fuse. ____True____

4. A circuit breaker has a switch that works like a fuse. ____True____

5. When a circuit breaker breaks a circuit, it has to be replaced. ____False____

B. Use the words below to complete the sentences.

breakers	fuse	lightning
circuit	heat	safe

1. ____Lightning____ can cause too much current in a circuit.

2. A ____fuse____ is like a little light bulb.

3. Every ____circuit____ usually has its own fuse.

4. Circuit ____breakers____ are sometimes used instead of fuses.

5. Fuses and circuit breakers help make electricity ____safe____ to use.

C. Write the letter for the correct answer.

1. When electricity flows through a circuit, some electricity changes into ____b____ .
   (a) steam   (b) heat   (c) smoke

2. When there is too much current in a circuit, the wires of the circuit get very ____a____ .
   (a) hot   (b) cool   (c) hard

Dry Cells and Batteries

Dry Cell

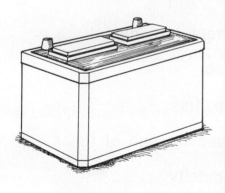

A Battery for a Car

If you have a television set at home, it is easy to make it work. You just plug the end of the electric cord into an outlet and turn on the TV. The electric current you need comes from the outlets in your home.

But when you are away from home, there may not be electric outlets around. Where do you get electricity to run your radio or your flashlight? **Dry cells** and **batteries** store electricity. If you have a dry cell or a battery, you can take electric energy with you wherever you go.

Dry cells are not really dry. The outside of one kind of dry cell is made of the metal zinc. Inside the cell is a paste of chemicals. The chemicals react with the zinc, which loses some electrons. As the chemicals react, a flow of electrons forms an electric current. So chemical energy becomes electric energy.

A dry cell has two posts called **terminals.** One terminal is positive. The other is negative. A wire can be put between the terminals to make a circuit. You can make something that uses electricity, such as a light bulb, a part of the circuit. The flow of electric current will light the bulb.

Some cells use a liquid instead of a paste between lead and zinc plates. Two or more of these cells can be connected to make a battery. The more cells in a battery, the more volts and current it can give. This type of battery is used in cars. The battery is used to start the engine.

A. Write the letter for the correct answer.

1. Dry cells and batteries store ____a____ .
   (a) electricity   (b) mechanical energy   (c) outlets

2. Inside a dry cell is a paste of ____c____ .
   (a) metals   (b) batteries   (c) chemicals

3. Chemicals in dry cells react with zinc to make ____b____ .
   (a) terminals   (b) electricity   (c) more dry cells

4. A dry cell has two posts called ____c____ .
   (a) outlets   (b) electric currents   (c) terminals

5. The more cells in a battery, the more volts and ____b____ it can give.
   (a) energy   (b) current   (c) engine

6. A battery in a car gives the current to ____c____ .
   (a) make the car run   (b) ring a bell   (c) start the engine

B. Use each word to write a sentence about dry cells and batteries.

1. terminals _____ Sentences will vary. _____

   _____

2. volts _____

   _____

C. Answer True or False.

1. At home, the electric current you need comes from outlets.
   ___True___

2. Dry cells are really dry. ___False___

3. A wire can be put between the terminals of a dry cell to make a
   circuit. ___True___

4. All cells use paste between lead and zinc plates. ___False___

5. One terminal of a dry cell is positive and the other is negative.
   ___True___

What Is Magnetism?

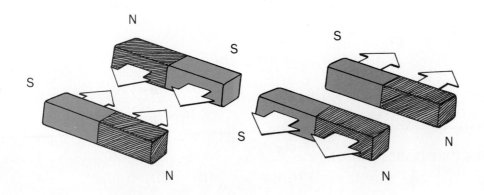

Different poles attract, and the same poles repel.

What keeps a refrigerator door closed? Most refrigerator doors are kept closed by **magnetism.** Magnetism is a pulling force that certain metals have. These metals, called **magnets,** attract and repel other pieces of metal. Attract means that two objects pull toward each other. Repel means that two objects push away from each other.

All magnets have two ends called **poles.** Each magnet has a north pole and a south pole. The north pole of one magnet attracts the south pole of another magnet. But the north pole of one magnet repels the north pole of another magnet. Two south poles also repel each other.

In some ways, Earth acts like a magnet with two poles. You can tell by using a magnetic compass. A magnetic compass is an instrument with a magnetized needle. One end of the needle always points to the magnetic north pole of Earth. Sailors use compasses to tell what direction they are going.

Magnets do not have to touch a piece of metal to attract it. There is an attracting area around every magnet called the **magnetic field.** When a piece of metal comes near a magnet, it is attracted by the magnetic field. The attraction gets stronger as the metal gets closer to the magnet.

A. Draw >—< to show when two magnetic poles attract. Draw <——> to show when two magnetic poles repel.

1. north pole ___>—<___ south pole

2. south pole ___<——>___ south pole

3. south pole ___>—<___ north pole

4. north pole ___<——>___ north pole

B. Use the words below to complete the sentences.

Attract	Magnetism	Repel
compass	metal	stronger
magnetic field	poles	weaker

1. _____Magnetism_____ is a pulling force that certain metals have.

2. Magnets attract and repel other pieces of _____metal_____.

3. _____Repel_____ means that two objects push away from each other.

4. _____Attract_____ means that two objects pull toward each other.

5. All magnets have two ends called _____poles_____.

6. You can tell that Earth acts like a magnet by using a magnetic _____compass_____.

7. There is an attracting area around magnets called the _____magnetic field_____.

8. The attraction of a piece of metal gets _____stronger_____ as the metal gets closer to the magnet.

C. Answer the question.

What is magnetism? _____Magnetism is a pulling force that_____
_____certain metals have._____

Electromagnets

As long as the electricity is turned on, an electromagnet can lift tons of metal.

You have learned that a magnet has a magnetic field around it. This field is the area in which the magnet acts on other objects. Magnetism is <u>related</u> to electricity. When electricity flows through a wire, it makes a magnetic field around the wire.

Suppose an electric wire is bent into a <u>coil</u>. When electricity flows through the wire, a magnetic field forms around the whole coil. The coil becomes a kind of magnet. It has north and south poles, just like a magnet.

If an iron bar is placed inside a coil of wire when electricity flows through it, an **electromagnet** is formed. An electromagnet is a much more powerful magnet than a coil of wire alone. When more wire is looped around the iron, the electromagnet becomes even stronger.

Doorbells are made from a tiny electromagnet. A large electromagnet is so powerful it can lift tons of iron. It can lift cars in junkyards, and even trains. But as soon as the flow of electricity is turned off, an electromagnet loses its magnetism. Then it drops whatever it was holding.

Not only can electricity make magnetic fields, magnetic fields can make electricity. If a magnet is moved in and out of a coil of copper wire, electricity begins to flow through the coil. This way of making electricity is called **electromagnetic induction.** Generators, which supply electricity, make their electricity by electromagnetic induction.

A. Answer True or False.

1. Magnetic fields can make electricity. ___True___

2. Electricity cannot make magnetic fields. ___False___

3. As soon as the flow of electricity is turned off, an electromagnet gets stronger. ___False___

4. If a magnet is moved in and out of a coil of copper wire, electricity begins to flow through the coil. ___True___

B. Fill in the missing words.

1. Magnetism is related to ___electricity___. (electricity, fuses)

2. A magnet has a magnetic field ___around___ it. (inside, around)

3. When electricity flows through a wire, ___a magnetic field___ forms around the wire. (electromagnetic induction, a magnetic field)

4. If an electric wire is bent into a ___coil___, and electricity flows through it, the coil becomes a kind of magnet. (square, coil)

5. If an iron bar is placed inside a coil of wire when electricity flows through it, ___an electromagnet___ is formed. (an electromagnet, a wire)

6. An electromagnet is a much ___more___ powerful magnet than a coil of wire alone. (more, less)

7. Generators make electricity by ___electromagnetic induction___. (electromagnetic induction, magnets)

C. Use each pair of words to write a sentence about electromagnets.

1. iron bar ___Sentences will vary.___ _____

_____

2. copper coil _____

_____

Electric Motors and Generators

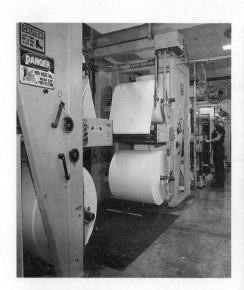

This printing press is run by an electric motor.

Whether you know it or not, there are electric motors all over your home. Electric motors are in clocks, in hair dryers, and in record players. They are in air conditioners, refrigerators, and washing machines. Outside your home, there are much bigger electric motors in many kinds of machines, such as trains and printing presses.

What is an electric motor? An electric motor is a machine that changes electric energy into mechanical energy. As you know, mechanical energy is needed to make anything move.

Electric motors use electromagnets and regular magnets. An electric current passed through the electromagnet keeps changing directions. This makes the poles of the electromagnet change. The north pole becomes the south pole, and the south pole becomes the north pole. Because of this change, its north pole is always lined up with the north pole of the regular magnet. The two north poles repel, making the electromagnet keep turning. As the electromagnet turns, it turns a rod that can run a machine. Belts can be attached to the rod. The belts can move machine parts.

In today's world, it is difficult to find a machine that is not run by an electric motor. A car uses an electric motor to start its engine. Once the engine is running, a belt is used to run a generator. The generator makes current to keep the engine running and to recharge the car's battery.

A. **Make a list of six machines that are run by electric motors.**

Answers may vary, but could include: electric

clock, hair dryer, record player, air conditioner,

refrigerator, washing machine, trains, and

printing presses.

B. **Fill in the missing words.**

1. An electric motor is a machine that changes electric energy into
   __mechanical__ energy. (mechanical, solar)

2. __Mechanical__ energy is needed to make anything move.
   (Motor, Mechanical)

3. Electric motors use electromagnets and __regular magnets__.
   (regular magnets, generators)

4. The electromagnet in an electric motor keeps changing __direction__.
   (size, direction)

5. A car's generator makes current to keep the engine running and to
   recharge the car's __battery__ . (engine, battery)

C. **Answer the questions.**

1. What is an electric motor? __An electric motor is a machine__
   __that changes electric energy into mechanical__
   __energy.__

2. What do electric motors use? __Electric motors use__
   __electromagnets and regular magnets.__

3. In an electric motor, what is the north pole of the electromagnet always
   lined up with? __It is always lined up with the__
   __north pole of the regular magnet.__

Electronics

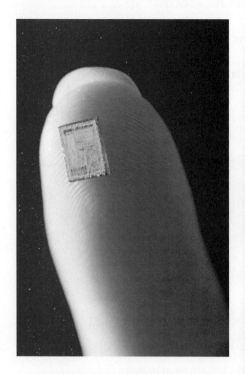

A microchip can have hundreds of transistors and other electronic devices.

Electronics is the branch of science that makes things such as radios, stereos, televisions, calculators, and computers. You have learned about machines that use electricity for energy. But electronic devices use electricity in another way. Electronic devices change electricity into signals. These signals can <u>represent</u> sounds, pictures, and numbers.

Transistors are tiny devices used to change current electricity into signals. Transistors do three main jobs. Some transistors change alternating current into direct current. All electronic devices use direct current. Other transistors make signals stronger. A third kind of transistor changes the signal's frequency.

A regular electric current flows through a conductor. But the current in electronic devices flows through a **semiconductor.** A semiconductor is a kind of matter that is not a very good conductor or insulator. But it can control an electric current. Many electronic devices use the semiconductor **silicon.**

You may have heard of **microchips.** The chips are so small, a microscope is needed to see their details. The chips are made of a thin slice of silicon. Instead of using wires, the circuits are etched on the chip.

Today, microchips are used in most electronic devices. Digital wrist watches are run by a single chip. Computers use chips that contain hundreds of thousands of parts. Chips can handle millions of pieces of information in one second.

A. Use the words below to complete the sentences.

different	microchips	silicon
direct	semiconductor	transistors
Electronics	signals	

1. _____Electronics_____ is the branch of science that makes things such as radios, televisions, calculators, and computers.

2. Electronic devices change electricity into _____signals_____.

3. Electronic devices use _____transistors_____ to change current electricity into signals.

4. All electronic devices use _____direct_____ current.

5. The current in electronic devices flows through a _____semiconductor_____.

6. Many electronic devices use the semiconductor _____silicon_____.

B. Answer <u>True</u> or <u>False</u>.

1. Electronic devices use electricity only for energy. ___False___

2. Electronic devices can change electricity into signals that can represent sounds, pictures, or numbers. ___True___

3. All electronic devices use direct current. ___True___

4. Microchips use tiny wires for circuits. ___False___

5. A semiconductor can control an electric current. ___True___

C. Answer the question.

What are the three main jobs that transistors do? ___They change___ _____alternating current to direct current. They make signals_____ _____stronger. They change the signal's frequency._____

Using Electricity Safely

Cover an outlet when it is not being used.

Machines run by electricity make life easier. But any machine or tool run by electricity must be used safely. Electricity can be dangerous.

People should take care when using electric outlets. Outlets are meant for plugging in electric cords only. Never put anything else into an electric outlet. An object put into an outlet can carry electricity. Electricity can burn the hand of the person holding the object. When cleaning or fixing an appliance, be sure to pull the plug out of the outlet. An appliance that is still plugged in can give a bad shock.

Water is a good conductor of electricity. Keep electric appliances away from water. For example, never wash or bathe with a hair dryer near you. If the appliance fell into the water, the electric shock could kill you instantly.

Answer the questions.

1. Why should you not keep a radio near a person bathing? _____
   _____If the appliance fell into the water, the electric_____
   _____shock could kill the bather instantly._____

2. Why should you never put anything other than a plug into an
   outlet? _____An object put into an outlet can carry electricity_____
   _____that can burn the hand of the person holding the object._____

UNIT 5 Review

Part A

Fill in the missing words.

1. Magnetism is a pulling force that certain metals, called

   _____magnets_____ , have. (compasses, magnets)

2. If an iron bar is placed inside a coil of wire when electricity flows

   through it, an _____electromagnet_____ is formed.
   (electric generator, electromagnet)

3. Electronic devices change electricity into ____signals____. (signals, volts)

4. The path taken by an electric current is called

   _____an electric circuit_____. (a volt, an electric circuit)

5. An electric motor is a machine that changes electric energy into

   ____mechanical____ energy. (chemical, mechanical)

6. Dry cells and batteries store _____electricity_____.
   (magnetism, electricity)

7. To keep fires from starting, ____fuses____ are put in circuits. (volts, fuses)

Part B

Read each sentence. Write <u>True</u> if the sentence is true. Write <u>False</u> if the sentence is false.

1. A volt measures the amount of push a source of electricity gives

   the electricity. ____True____

2. The north pole of one magnet attracts the north pole of another

   magnet. ____False____

3. The more cells that are in a battery, the more volts and current it

   can give. ____True____

4. Electrons can easily move through an insulator. ____False____

5. Electric motors use electromagnets and regular magnets. ____True____

Make a Magnetic Racer

You Need

- a partner
- cork
- small paper clip
- rectangular plastic pan
- water
- bar magnet

1. Take a round slice of cork $\frac{1}{8}$ to $\frac{1}{4}$ inches thick. Stick a paper clip on it as shown in the top picture. This is your magnetic racer.

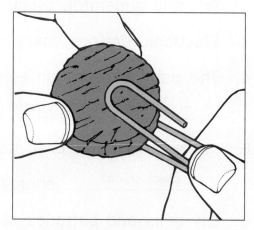

2. Now work with a classmate. Get a plastic pan and fill it with water.

3. Get ready to have a race! Both of you should put your magnetic racers at one end of the pan as shown in the bottom picture.

4. Have your magnets handy. When one of you says, "Ready, set, go!" use the magnet to move your racer to the other side of the pan without touching the racer.

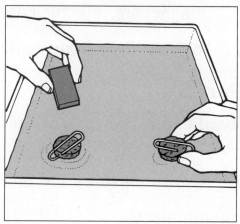

5. Be careful! If your racer sticks to your magnet, you will have to start over. The first racer to get to the other side of the pan without touching the magnet wins.

Write the Answer

How can the magnet attract and move the racer without touching it?

A magnet is surrounded by

a magnetic field. The magnetic field can

attract metal objects such as the racer.

Fill in the circle in front of the word or phrase that best completes each sentence. The first one is done for you.

1. Short circuits can
   - ⓐ make a closed circuit.
   - ● start fires.
   - ⓒ make an open circuit.

2. The current in electronic devices flows through
   - ⓐ a semiconductor.
   - ⓑ a conductor.
   - ⓒ an insulator.

3. Electric motors change electric energy into
   - ⓐ magnetism.
   - ⓑ chemical energy.
   - ⓒ mechanical energy.

4. Generators make electricity by
   - ⓐ circuit breakers.
   - ⓑ electric outlets.
   - ⓒ electromagnetic induction.

5. The attracting area around every magnet is
   - ⓐ electricity.
   - ⓑ a magnetic field.
   - ⓒ a terminal.

6. People should take care when using
   - ⓐ electric outlets.
   - ⓑ magnetism.
   - ⓒ compasses.

Fill in the missing words.

7. A dry cell has two posts called ____terminals____. (terminals, circuits)

8. The amount of push a source of electricity gives the electricity is measured in ____volts____. (circuits, volts)

9. Tons of iron can be lifted by ____electromagnets____. (fuses, electromagnets)

Write the answer on the lines.

10. What kind of current is provided by the electric outlets in your house?

   Alternating current is provided

   by the electric outlets in a house.

UNIT 6
Motion and Forces

Has this car moved?

Has this car moved?

What Is Motion?

Suppose you are looking out a window. You see a car going by. The car is in **motion**. In motion means moving. But how do you really know the car is in motion?

Look at pictures 1 and 2 on this page. In picture 1, the car is to the right of the tree. In picture 2, after 2 seconds, the car is to the left of the tree. The tree cannot move from one place to another. So the car must have moved from one place to another. The car must have been in motion.

Now look at pictures 3 and 4. Picture 3 and picture 4 are 2 seconds apart. Did the car move? You cannot tell. You cannot tell whether an object is in motion unless you have a **frame of reference.** A frame of reference is some other object to which you compare an object's position. In this case, you have no frame of reference. So you cannot tell whether the car is in motion. An object is in motion only in relation to other objects.

Have you ever ridden on an airplane at night? If you have, you know that you do not feel like the plane is moving. Unless you can see lights from the window, you have no frame of reference. You know the plane is in motion in relation to Earth. But you feel as though the plane were still.

Scientists always use a frame of reference to talk about motion. For example, when they study the motion of stars in the sky, they use other stars as a frame of reference. Only in this way can they know the stars are moving.

A. Answer True or False.

1. In motion means moving. _____True_____

2. Scientists do not use a frame of reference to talk about motion. _____False_____

3. You cannot tell whether an object is in motion unless you have a frame of reference. _____True_____

4. A frame of reference is some other object to which you compare an object's position. _____True_____

5. When scientists study the motion of stars in the sky, they use clouds as a frame of reference. _____False_____

B. Answer the questions.

1   2   3

 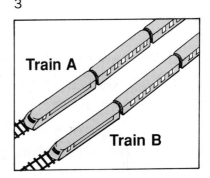

1. Look at picture 1 and then at picture 2, which was taken later. Is the train in motion? _____Yes_____

2. How do you know? _____It is in a different place in relation to the background._____

3. Which is the frame of reference, the train or the countryside? _____
   The countryside is the frame of reference._____

4. In picture 3, can you tell if train A is in motion? _____No_____

5. In picture 3, can you tell if train B is in motion? _____No_____

6. Explain your answers to questions 4 and 5. _____There is no frame of reference to compare the motion to._____

97

Speed, Velocity, and Acceleration

If the direction of motion changes, velocity changes.

If the speed of motion changes, velocity also changes.

You know a car is in motion if you see it in one place and then in another place, in relation to an object. Motion can change in several ways.

One thing that can change about motion is its **speed.** Speed is the distance something moves in a certain time. Many people can walk 2 miles in 1 hour. Their speed is 2 miles per hour. It is written 2 miles/hour. Some people can run 7 miles an hour, or 7 miles/hour. The speed of 7 miles/hour is faster than 2 miles/hour.

Another thing that can change about motion is its **velocity.** Velocity is speed in a certain direction. If you are running at 7 miles/hour along a straight path, your velocity is the same as your speed. But if you are running around a track, you are changing your direction. So your speed is the same, but your velocity is changing. Velocity changes when the direction of the motion changes.

You can also change your velocity by changing your speed. This change in velocity is called **acceleration.** If you pedal a bicycle so that it speeds up, that is positive acceleration. If you use the brakes to slow down, that is negative acceleration.

A. Use the words below to complete the sentences.

acceleration	negative	speed
motion	positive	velocity

1. The distance something moves in a certain time is _____speed_____ .

2. Speed in a certain direction is _____velocity_____ .

3. A change in velocity is _____acceleration_____ .

4. If motion speeds up, it is _____positive_____ acceleration.

5. If motion slows down, it is _____negative_____ acceleration.

B. Underline the correct words.

1. You know a car is (accelerating, <u>in motion</u>) if you see it in one place and then in another place.

2. You can change your velocity by changing your (<u>speed</u>, distance).

3. Motion can change in (one way, <u>several ways</u>).

4. If you use brakes on a bicycle to slow down, that is negative (<u>acceleration</u>, velocity).

C. Answer the questions.

1. What is the difference between positive and negative acceleration?

   _____Speeding up is positive acceleration. Slowing down_____

   _____is negative acceleration._____

2. What is speed? _____Speed is the distance something_____

   _____moves in a certain time._____

3. In what two ways can velocity be changed? _____Velocity changes when_____

   _____the direction of motion changes. You can also change velocity_____

   _____by changing your speed._____

Balanced and Unbalanced Forces

Suppose your teacher asked you to move a heavy desk in your classroom. How would you move it? You might get on one side of the desk and start pushing. Or you might grab the legs and start pulling. Either way, you would be using a **force.** Any push or pull is a force.

The force you use in pushing or pulling the desk has a size. You could use a small amount of force or a lot of force. Forces <u>differ</u> in size. Another way forces differ is in direction. A force can be left or right, or up or down.

The desk will not move by itself. A force is needed to put the desk in motion. But even when the desk is not moving, forces are acting on it. The floor is actually pushing up on the desk. At the same time, the force of gravity is pulling down on it. If the desk is not in motion, the upward push is the same as the downward pull. The size of the forces is the same, but the directions of the forces are different. Whenever forces are the same in size but opposite in direction, they are <u>balanced</u> forces. An object that is not in motion will never move if balanced forces act on it.

How can you move the desk? You can move it because you <u>unbalance</u> the forces. The size of your force is greater than the force of air pushing on the other side of the desk. Unbalanced forces act in opposite directions but differ in size. If unbalanced forces act on an object, the object will always move in the direction of the greater force.

A. Answer True or False.

1. Any push or pull is a force. _____True_____

2. Forces do not differ in direction. _____False_____

3. A force is needed to put things in motion. _____True_____

4. When an object is not moving, forces are not acting on it.
   _____False_____

5. Forces different in size but the same in direction are balanced
   forces. _____False_____

6. Unbalanced forces act in opposite directions but differ in size.
   _____True_____

B. Answer the questions.

1. Why does a heavy desk not move by itself? _____A force is needed_____
   _____to put it in motion._____

2. When a heavy desk is not moving, what kind of forces are acting
   on it? _____The floor is pushing up on the desk. The force of_____
   _____gravity is pulling down on it._____

3. If unbalanced forces act on a desk, the desk will always move in
   which direction? _____It will move in the direction_____
   _____of the greater force._____

C. Write the letter for the correct answer.

1. An object that is not in motion will _____c_____ move if balanced
   forces act on it.
   (a) always   (b) sometimes   (c) never

2. You can move an object because you _____c_____.
   (a) balance gravity   (b) balance forces   (c) unbalance forces

3. Forces differ in _____c_____.
   (a) size only   (b) direction only   (c) size and direction

101

Gravity

The same force of gravity makes dead leaves fall to the ground and keeps the moon moving in a circle around Earth.

Gravity is a force that <u>attracts</u>, or pulls on, matter. On Earth, gravity attracts all matter to the ground. Leaves from a tree, raindrops, or a ball you throw in the air are all pulled to the ground by Earth's force of gravity.

Earth is not the only object that has gravity. All matter has gravity. The more mass matter has, the greater the force of its gravity. Earth has a great amount of mass. So the gravity of Earth itself is stronger than the gravity of anything on Earth. It is the pull of Earth's gravity that gives weight to all matter on Earth. How much you weigh is the amount of pull on the mass of your body.

The moon has gravity. Since the moon has less mass than Earth, it has less gravity. The moon's gravity is about one sixth as strong as Earth's. Why doesn't the motion of the moon make the moon fly off into space? The greater force of Earth's gravity pulls the moon. So instead of flying off into space or being pulled to Earth, the moon keeps moving in a circle around Earth.

All the other planets have gravity, too. So does the sun. Since the sun's gravity is the strongest, it pulls on all the planets. The planets keep moving in a circle around the sun.

A. **Fill in the missing words.**

1. Gravity is a force that ____attracts____ matter. (attracts, repels)

2. On Earth, gravity attracts all matter to the ____ground____.
   (sky, ground)

3. The more mass matter has, the ____greater____ the force of its gravity. (less, greater)

4. Earth's gravity gives ____weight____ to matter. (weight, mass)

5. The moon ____has____ gravity. (has, does not have)

B. **Mark with an X each happening that is caused by gravity.**

1. A bulb in a lamp lights up. _____

2. You weigh more than a baby. ____X____

3. The moon moves in a circle around Earth. ____X____

4. Birds sing. _____

5. A ball thrown in the air falls to the ground. ____X____

C. **Use each word to write a sentence about gravity.**

1. force _____Sentences will vary._____

   _____

2. weight _____

   _____

3. planets _____

   _____

D. **Answer the question.**

Why does the moon have less gravity than Earth? _____

_____Since the moon has less mass than Earth, it_____

_____has less gravity._____

Laws of Motion

If forces are balanced, an object at rest will stay at rest until . . .

the forces become unbalanced.

About 300 years ago, a scientist named Isaac Newton had some ideas about forces and motion. His ideas became known as Newton's laws of motion. They are called laws because they correctly explain certain happenings around you.

One of Newton's laws says that if all the forces acting on an object are balanced, the object will keep its state of motion. In other words, if the object is at rest, or not moving, it will stay at rest. If the object is moving, it will keep on moving. The state of motion will stay the same unless the forces become unbalanced by some other force.

Suppose you see a soccer ball on the grass. It is at rest. The force of the ground pushing up on it is balanced by the force of gravity pulling down on it. The soccer ball will keep its state of motion, which in this case is no motion. Suppose you kick the ball. You have unbalanced the forces with the force of your kick. The ball will be in motion. The ball will stay in motion until some other force comes along. In this case, a force called <u>friction</u> will stop the ball after a while.

Another law of motion says that for every action there is an equal and opposite <u>reaction</u>. When a rocket is launched, burning fuel makes hot gases come out of the bottom of the rocket. The gases push on the rocket. The rocket pushes on the gases and takes off, moving away from Earth. The gases pushing the rocket is the action. The rocket moving up is the reaction.

A. **Use the words below to complete the sentences.**

action	gravity	reaction
balanced	laws	unbalanced

1. Isaac Newton's ideas about forces and motion became known as Newton's _____ laws _____ of motion.

2. If all the forces acting on an object are _____ balanced _____, the object will keep its state of motion.

3. The state of motion will stay the same until the forces become _____ unbalanced _____ by some other force.

4. The force of the ground pushing up on an object at rest is balanced by the force of _____ gravity _____ pulling down on it.

5. For every action, there is an equal and opposite _____ reaction _____.

B. **Write the word or words that best finish each sentence.**

1. If an object is at rest, it will stay at _____ rest _____.

2. If an object is moving, it will continue _____ moving _____.

3. For every _____ action _____, there is an equal and opposite reaction.

C. **Answer True or False.**

1. An object will keep its state of motion if the forces acting on it are unbalanced. _____ False _____

2. The law of action and reaction explains how a rocket takes off from Earth. _____ True _____

3. If you kick a soccer ball that is at rest, you have balanced the forces acting on it. _____ False _____

4. Friction will stop a moving ball after a while. _____ True _____

Space Travel

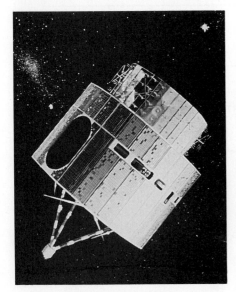

A Weather Satellite

Scientists use what they know about forces and motion when they send rockets into space. Gravity pulls things toward Earth. In order to lift rockets into space, powerful engines are needed. The force of the rocket engines must be greater than the force of gravity. In that way the rockets can escape Earth's powerful pull.

Some rockets carry **satellites.** Once a satellite is in space, the force from its engine balances the force from Earth's gravity. Then the satellite circles Earth the way the moon circles Earth. Some satellites are put into space to study the weather on Earth. Other satellites send radio and television signals around the world. Some rockets explore other planets and their natural satellites, or moons.

A. **Answer the questions.**

1. What do scientists need to know about to send rockets into space?

   To send rockets into space, scientists need

   to know about forces and motion.

2. What pulls things toward Earth? Gravity pulls things

   toward Earth.

3. What are needed to lift rockets into space? Powerful engines are

   needed to lift rockets into space.

B. **Answer True or False.**

1. Rockets do not carry satellites. False

2. Some satellites study weather on Earth. True

3. Some rockets explore other planets. True

106

Part A

Write the letter for the correct answer.

1. You cannot tell whether there is motion unless you have a _____b_____.
   (a) picture   (b) frame of reference   (c) window

2. Speed is the distance something moves in a certain _____c_____.
   (a) direction   (b) velocity   (c) time

3. Velocity is speed in a certain _____a_____.
   (a) direction   (b) distance   (c) time

4. Any push or pull is _____b_____.
   (a) gravity   (b) a force   (c) matter

5. Forces differ in size and _____c_____.
   (a) speed   (b) distance   (c) direction

6. Gravity is a force that attracts _____a_____.
   (a) matter   (b) energy   (c) weight

7. If forces acting on an object are balanced, the object will keep its state

   of _____a_____.
   (a) motion   (b) gravity   (c) matter

8. For every action, there is an equal and opposite _____c_____.
   (a) direction   (b) weight   (c) reaction

Part B

Read each sentence. Write <u>True</u> if the sentence is true. Write <u>False</u> if the sentence is false.

1. A change in velocity is called acceleration. _____True_____

2. Whenever forces are the same in size but opposite in direction, they

   are balanced forces. _____True_____

3. An object is in motion only in relation to other objects. _____True_____

4. A force is never needed to put things in motion. _____False_____

5. Earth's gravity gives weight to all matter on Earth. _____True_____

Make a Balloon Rocket

You Need

- a partner
- string (length of classroom)
- straw
- masking tape
- balloon

1. Work in pairs. Push the string through the straw.

2. Tie the string to objects on opposite sides of the room. For example, you could tie it to the backs of two chairs. The string should be stretched tight. The straw should be at one end of the string.

3. One person should blow up the balloon and hold it so that no air can escape.

4. The person with the balloon should hold it under the straw. The other person should tape the balloon to the straw. The tape should go over the top of the straw as shown in the picture.

5. Let go of the balloon. It will take off like a rocket.

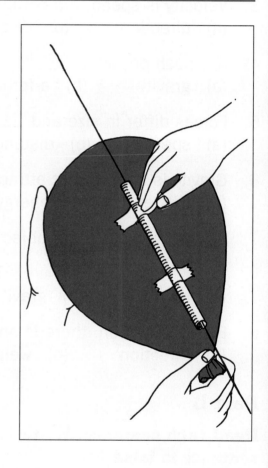

Write the Answer

When the balloon rocket flies across the room, what is pushing on what? What law of motion does this show?

The air pushes on the balloon and the balloon

pushes on the air. This shows that for every

action there is an equal and opposite reaction.

Fill in the circle in front of the word or phrase that best completes each sentence. The first one is done for you.

1. For every action there is an equal and opposite
   - ● reaction.
   - ⓑ velocity.
   - ⓒ frame of reference.

2. Isaac Newton's ideas became known as the laws of
   - ⓐ speed.
   - **ⓑ** motion.
   - ⓒ acceleration.

3. If you pedal a bicycle so that it speeds up, that is
   - ⓐ velocity.
   - **ⓑ** positive acceleration.
   - ⓒ negative acceleration.

4. Unbalanced forces act in opposite directions but differ in
   - ⓐ time.
   - ⓑ distance.
   - **ⓒ** size.

5. An object at rest
   - **ⓐ** will stay at rest.
   - ⓑ will start moving.
   - ⓒ is unbalanced.

6. The more mass matter has the greater the force of its
   - ⓐ frame of reference.
   - ⓑ motion.
   - **ⓒ** gravity.

Fill in the missing words.

7. Gravity is a _____ force _____ that attracts matter.
   (motion, force)

8. Any push or pull is _____ a force _____. (gravity, a force)

9. Motion depends on a _____ frame of reference _____.
   (frame of reference, reaction)

Write the answer on the lines.

10. What does the pull of Earth's gravity give to all matter on Earth?

The pull of Earth's gravity
_____

gives weight to all matter on Earth.
_____

109

UNIT 7
Machines

What Is Work?

This box is being moved. Is work being done?

You probably do many kinds of work. You may do work for school. You may do work around your house, such as mowing the lawn. You may work at a job. But these things are not what scientists call work. For scientists, work has a special meaning.

For scientists, **work** is the use of force to move an object. In order for an action to be work, the force used must be in the same direction as the motion.

If you pushed as hard as you could against a heavy desk and the desk did not move, you would not be doing work. Work only happens when an object moves.

Lifting a box is work. When you lift a box, you use a force to move the box. You pull upward on the box, and the box moves upward.

But carrying a box is not work. When you carry a box, you are using force to keep the box from falling. The force is an upward force. But the box is moving forward as you walk. The force and the motion are not in the same direction. So no work is being done.

In this unit you will learn more about work and how people make work easier to do.

A. Use the words below to complete the sentences.

direction	force	work

1. For scientists, _____work_____ has a special meaning.

2. Work is the use of _____force_____ to move an object.

3. In order for an action to be work, the force used must be in the same _____direction_____ as the motion.

B. Answer <u>True</u> or <u>False</u>.

1. Scientists would call watching TV work. _____False_____

2. If you pushed as hard as you could against a heavy desk, and the desk didn't move, you would be doing work. _____False_____

3. Work only happens when an object moves. _____True_____

4. Lifting a box is not work. _____False_____

5. Carrying a box is not work because the force and the motion are not in the same direction. _____True_____

6. When you lift a box, you pull upward on the box, and the box moves downward. _____False_____

C. Use each word to write a sentence about work.

1. force _____ Sentences will vary. _____

_____

2. motion _____

_____

3. direction _____

_____

111

Friction

Friction is the rubbing of one object against another. It is a force that <u>resists</u>, or works against, motion. It slows down moving objects. Every motion that takes place on Earth is affected by friction. Without friction, life would be very different.

You could not walk without friction to keep your feet from sliding on the ground. Concrete, grass, and dirt are rough surfaces. Rough surfaces <u>provide</u> more friction than smooth surfaces. If you have ever tried to walk on ice, you know that your feet slip and slide. Smooth surfaces such as ice provide very little friction.

Without friction, you could not pick things up and hold them. Everything you tried to hold would slip through your hands and fall.

Without friction, cars could not move. Their tires would not hold on to the road. When a car gets stuck in mud, the wheels turn around, but the car does not move. Mud does not provide enough friction for the tires to hold.

Have you ever tried to push a heavy box? Friction between the ground and the box makes this difficult. You can make the box easier to push by taking some things out of the box. This makes the box lighter. The heavier something is, the more friction slows it down.

Friction makes heat. Try rubbing your hands together. You will feel them getting warmer. When you rub two sticks together, they get warmer and warmer. When they get hot enough, they start to burn.

Friction keeps you from slipping.

A. Use the words below to complete the sentences.

friction	little	resists
heat	motion	

1. The rubbing of one object against another is ___friction___ .

2. Friction is a force that ___resists___ , or works against, motion.

3. Every ___motion___ that takes place on Earth is affected by friction.

4. Smooth surfaces such as ice provide very ___little___ friction.

5. Friction makes ___heat___ .

B. Underline the correct words.

1. Friction keeps your feet from (walking, <u>sliding</u>) on the ground.

2. The heavier something is, the more friction (<u>slows it down</u>, speeds it up).

3. If you rub your hands together, you will feel them getting (<u>warm</u>, cold).

4. Without friction, life would be (the same, <u>very different</u>).

5. Friction makes it (<u>difficult</u>, easy) to push heavy objects along the ground.

C. For motions which friction helps, write **H**. For motions which friction makes difficult, write **D**.

1. pushing a heavy box ___D___

2. picking things up ___H___

3. walking ___H___

4. driving a car ___H___

5. making a fire ___H___

What Are Machines?

A wagon is a machine that cuts down on friction.

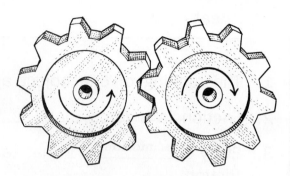

Gears can change the direction of a force.

It is easier to pull a large rock in a wagon than to push it on the ground. It is easier to tighten a nut with a wrench than with your fingers. It is easier to raise a car with a jack than to lift it yourself. A wagon, a wrench, and a jack are all machines. Machines make work easier.

Some machines cut down on friction. Others can change the amount of force used. Still others can change the direction of a force. Gears can do this. Some machines do more than one of these things.

It is easier to pull a large rock in a wagon because the wagon's wheels cut down on friction. When the rock is on the ground, all of the rock that is touching the ground provides friction. When the rock is in the wagon, only the wheels touch the ground. The wheels use the friction with the ground to turn and move the rock.

It is easier to tighten a nut with a wrench because the wrench makes the amount of force larger. Another machine that changes the direction of force is a pulley. When you pull down on a drapery cord, the drapes open.

If there were no machines, you would have to walk everywhere. There would be no bicycles, cars, trains, buses, or planes. There would be no wagons or wheelbarrows to move things. It is hard to imagine what life would be like without machines.

A. Draw lines to match the machines with the work they can do for you.

1. wrench — tighten a nut
2. wagon — pull a large rock
3. jack — raise a car

B. Fill in the missing words.

1. Machines make work _____easier_____ . (easier, harder)

2. The wagon's wheels cut down on _____friction_____ . (speed, friction)

3. A wrench makes the amount of the force _____larger_____ . (larger, smaller)

4. A pulley changes the _____direction_____ of the force. (speed, direction)

5. It is _____easier_____ to raise a car with a jack than to lift it yourself. (easier, harder)

C. List three ways machines make work easier.

1. _____Some machines cut down on friction._____

2. _____Other machines can change the amount of force used._____

3. _____Still other machines can change the direction of the force used._____

D. Use each word in a sentence about machines.

1. force _____Sentences will vary._____

2. friction _____

Simple Machines

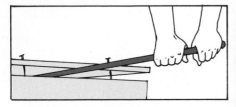

Lever

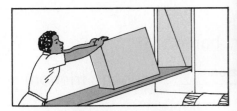

Inclined Plane

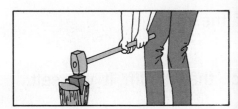

Wedge

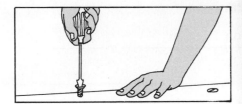

Screw

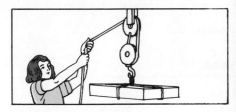

Pulley

Wheel and Axle

There are thousands of different kinds of machines. You use machines every day. But did you know that all machines are based on only six kinds of **simple machines?** The six simple machines are the **lever, inclined plane, wedge, screw, pulley,** and **wheel and axle.** Look at their pictures on this page.

A lever is a rod that can turn on a point called a **fulcrum.** If you push down on the end of one kind of lever, the other end moves up. You can lift things more easily because less force is needed. There are three basic kinds of levers. They are different because each kind has the fulcrum in a different place.

An inclined plane is a flat surface that slopes. A board from a low place to a high place is an inclined plane called a ramp. Less force is needed to slide an object up a ramp than to lift the object.

A wedge is two inclined planes that come together in a point. You can split a log more easily by hitting a wedge stuck in the log than by hitting the log with an ax. A screw is an inclined plane wrapped around a rod. Screws hold things together better than nails.

A pulley is a wheel with a rope around it. You can fasten an object to one end of the rope. If you pull the other end, you can lift the object. Several pulleys can be joined together to make it easy to lift heavy objects. A wheel and axle is really a kind of lever that continues to turn around its fulcrum.

A. **Use the words below to label each machine.**

| inclined plane | pulley | wedge |
| lever | screw | wheel and axle |

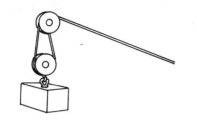

1. _____ pulley _____

4. _____ wedge _____

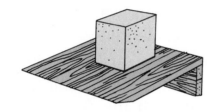

2. _____ inclined plane _____

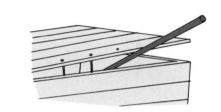

5. _____ lever _____

3. _____ screw _____

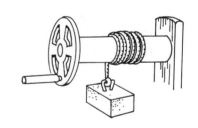

6. _____ wheel and axle _____

B. **Answer True or False.**

1. There are 12 kinds of simple machines. _____ False _____

2. A fulcrum is the point that a lever turns on. _____ True _____

3. Pulleys cannot be joined together. _____ False _____

4. Screws hold things together better than nails. _____ True _____

5. Less force is needed to slide an object up a ramp than to lift the object. _____ True _____

Compound Machines

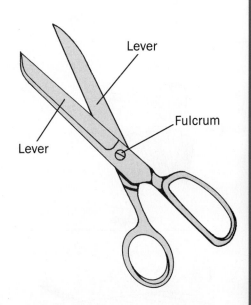

Lever

Fulcrum

Lever

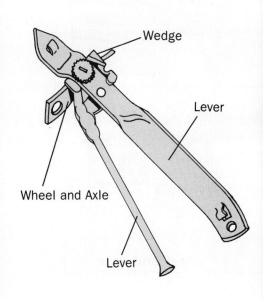

Wedge

Lever

Wheel and Axle

Lever

A compound machine is made of two or more simple machines.

Try pulling a nail out of wood with your fingers. It is very hard to do. But with the end of a claw hammer, it is easy to get the nail out. The hammer is a lever. It increases the force you put on the nail.

Compound machines can make work even easier than simple machines. A compound machine is a simple machine connected to one or more other simple machines. In a compound machine, the force you pass on to one simple machine is made larger and passed on to another simple machine. In this way, the total force is made much larger.

Compound machines are all around you. A scissors is a compound machine. It is simply two levers, with the fulcrum where the pin is. A can opener is a compound machine. The two handles are levers. The key you turn to open a can is a wheel and axle. The blade that cuts into the can is a wedge. A bicycle is another compound machine. Its wheels are connected to axles. So they make a wheel-and-axle machine. The brake handles are levers.

A machine cannot make energy. But every machine needs energy. When you pedal a bicycle, you provide the energy. Many machines use electric energy.

All machines waste energy. Remember that friction is a force that resists motion. Machines usually have moving parts that rub against each other. Friction slows down the motion of the parts. So energy is wasted. The work done by a machine is always less than the work put into it.

A. **Write the letter for the correct answer.**

1. A simple machine connected to one or more other simple
   machines is _____b_____ machine.
   (a) a big   (b) a compound   (c) an electric

2. In a compound machine, the total force is _____c_____ .
   (a) made much less   (b) the same   (c) made much larger

3. A machine cannot make _____c_____ .
   (a) products   (b) friction   (c) energy

4. Every machine needs _____a_____ .
   (a) energy   (b) friction   (c) electricity

5. The work done by a machine is always _____a_____ the work put into it.
   (a) less than   (b) the same as   (c) more than

B. **Answer True or False.**

1. When you pedal a bicycle, you provide the energy. _____True_____

2. Friction speeds up the motion of the parts of a machine.
   _____False_____

3. In a compound machine, the force put on one simple machine is
   made larger and put on another simple machine. _____True_____

4. All machines waste energy. _____True_____

5. Machines usually have moving parts that rub against each other.
   _____True_____

6. A scissors is a simple machine. _____False_____

7. Many machines use electric energy. _____True_____

C. **Use each word to write a sentence about compound machines.**

1. simple _____Sentences will vary._____

   _____

2. friction _____

   _____

119

Gasoline Engines

The Model T was a popular car in the early 1900s.

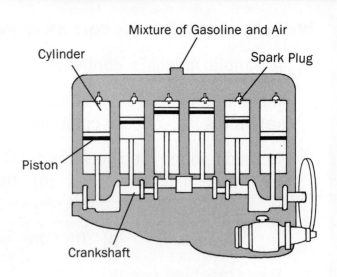

Gasoline Engine

A car is a compound machine. It is made up of many simple machines. One of the most important parts of a car is its **engine.** The engine is a compound machine, too. In most cars, the engine gets its energy from gasoline. Gasoline is a fuel. Engines that use gasoline as their fuel are called gasoline engines.

A gasoline engine has up to eight tubes called cylinders. The engine also has a carburetor where gasoline is mixed with air. The carburetor sends this mixture to the cylinders. Some gasoline engines do not have carburetors. Instead, a fuel-injection system squirts fuel into the cylinders.

Each cylinder has its own spark plug. When the mixture of gasoline and air reaches the tops of the cylinders, the spark plugs start little fires. The gases from the fires push on pistons inside the cylinders. The pistons move up and down.

The up-and-down motion of the pistons moves another part of the engine called the crankshaft. The motion of the crankshaft gives the energy the car needs for the wheels to turn and for the car to move.

Gasoline engines are not only used in cars. They can also be used in lawn mowers, small boats, trucks, and propeller airplanes.

A. The steps below describe how a gasoline engine makes a car move. Number the steps in the correct order. The first one is done for you.

_____3_____ The spark plugs start little fires.

_____6_____ The motion of the crankshaft makes the car move.

_____1_____ Gasoline mixes with air in the carburetor.

_____5_____ The motion of the pistons moves the crankshaft.

_____2_____ The mixture of gasoline and air reaches the tops of the cylinders.

_____4_____ Gases from the fires push on pistons inside cylinders.

B. Fill in the missing words.

1. A car is a _____compound_____ machine. (compound, simple)

2. The engine of a car is a _____compound_____ machine. (compound, simple)

3. In most cars, the engine gets its energy from _____gasoline_____. (air, gasoline)

4. Engines that use gasoline as their fuel are called _____gasoline engines_____. (compound machines, gasoline engines)

5. Gasoline engines are _____not only_____ used in cars. (only, not only)

C. Draw lines to complete the sentences.

1. Pistons   has its own spark plug.

2. Each cylinder   start little fires.

3. A gasoline engine   is a fuel.

4. Spark plugs   move up and down.

5. Gasoline   has up to eight cylinders.

D. Answer the question.

What are five machines that use gasoline engines? _____cars, lawn_____

_____mowers, small boats, trucks, and propeller airplanes_____

121

Jet Engines

Jet engines make it possible for this jet to fly.

Most large airplanes today are powered by jet engines. Jet engines are compound machines. How do jet engines work?

Air goes into the engine. A compressor squeezes the air, which is then mixed with fuel. The fuel mixture burns and produces hot gases. The gases turn a turbine wheel that runs the compressor. Then the gases rush out of the engine toward the tail of the plane.

Jet engines work because of one of the laws of motion. Remember that for every action there is an equal and opposite reaction. The action is gases rushing out of the engine. The reaction is the motion of the plane in the opposite direction. The gases do not need any matter to push against. Even without air, a jet plane would move.

Answer True or False.

1. Most large airplanes today are powered by jet engines. _____True_____

2. In a jet plane, hot gases rush out of the engine toward the front of the plane. _____False_____

3. As gases rush out of the plane's engine, the plane moves forward. _____True_____

122

Part A

Underline the correct words.

1. Work only happens when an object (falls, <u>moves</u>).

2. Carrying boxes is not work, because the force and the motion are not (<u>in the same direction</u>, at the same speed).

3. (Work, <u>Friction</u>) is a force that resists motion.

4. Rough surfaces provide (less, <u>more</u>) friction than smooth surfaces.

5. Machines make work (harder, <u>easier</u>).

6. All machines are based on six kinds of (<u>simple</u>, compound) machines.

7. (<u>Less</u>, More) force is needed to slide an object up a ramp than to lift the object.

8. A simple machine connected to one or more other simple machines is (an engine, <u>a compound machine</u>).

9. A machine (can, <u>cannot</u>) make energy.

10. A gasoline engine has up to eight tubes called (carburetors, <u>cylinders</u>).

11. The fuel mixture in a jet plane burns and produces (<u>hot gases</u>, air).

Part B

Read each sentence. Write <u>True</u> if the sentence is true. Write <u>False</u> if the sentence is false.

1. Friction makes heat. ____True____

2. A wedge is two levers that come together in a point. ____False____

3. A compound machine is made up of two or more simple machines.
____True____

4. Lifting a box is not work. ____False____

123

Find Out About Friction

You Need

- wood or heavy cardboard about 3 feet long
- tape
- box of crayons or other small object
- materials to cover the wood (cloth, sandpaper, waxed paper, etc.)
- stack of books
- watch with second hand

1. Work in small groups. Prop the wood up against a stack of books.

2. Put your object at the top. Time how long it takes the object to slide to the bottom.

3. Cover the wood with one of your materials. Keep the slope the same. Time how long it takes the object to slide now.

4. Cover the wood with a different material and repeat.

5. Make a bar graph that shows the time it took for your object to slide on each material. Compare your results with the results of your classmates.

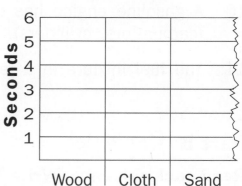

Write the Answer

Which material has the most friction? The least? How do you know?

The [sandpaper] had the most friction and the

[wood] had the least. The box slid the slowest on

the [sandpaper] and the fastest on the [wood].

Fill in the circle in front of the word or phrase that best completes each sentence. The first one is done for you.

1. Moving objects are slowed down by
   - ⓐ work.
   - ● friction.
   - ⓒ machines.

2. A wheel with a rope around it is
   - ⓐ a pulley.
   - ⓑ an inclined plane.
   - ⓒ a compound machine.

3. As hot gases leave a jet plane's engine, the plane
   - ⓐ stops.
   - ⓑ moves backward.
   - ⓒ moves forward.

4. All machines are based on only six kinds of
   - ⓐ work.
   - ⓑ simple machines.
   - ⓒ energy.

5. A machine cannot make
   - ⓐ energy.
   - ⓑ friction.
   - ⓒ heat.

6. The use of force to move an object is called
   - ⓐ energy.
   - ⓑ friction.
   - ⓒ work.

Fill in the missing words.

7. Work is made easier by _____machines_____.
   (forces, machines)

8. The point that a lever turns on is a _____fulcrum_____.
   (fulcrum, crankshaft)

9. Most cars use _____gasoline_____ engines. (jet, gasoline)

Write the answer on the lines.

10. Where do the engines in most cars get their energy?

   _____The engines in most cars_____

   _____get their energy from gasoline._____

UNIT 8
Technology

Monitor

Hard Disk

Keyboard

Computers

Computers are machines that store and work with information. But computers cannot think. Instructions called **programs**, or **software**, are put into the computers. A keyboard is used to type instructions for the computer to use.

A computer has a TV-like screen called a monitor. It shows what you type using the keyboard. It also shows stored information you want to find, read, or change. Most computers can be connected to a printer. Printers print information on paper.

All computers need an operating system program. This program is usually installed on a hard disk. Hard disks hold a lot of information. But the space for this information can get used up. Computers can also use small information disks called floppy disks, or other information disks called compact disks, or CDs. CDs hold more information than floppy disks. You can buy CDs with programs on them.

Some computers have a part called a modem. A modem connects a computer to the phone line. You can pay to join a network service. It will connect your computer to others all over the world. Some computers have sound and speakers. Some can use CD type disks called CD-ROM disks. These disks can store words, sound, and even pictures. You can watch TV or VCR tapes on some computers.

A. Write the letter for the correct answer.

1. Computers are machines that can store and work with ____a____ .
   (a) information   (b) objects   (c) light

2. Computers cannot ____a____ .
   (a) think   (b) use software   (c) store information

3. The instructions people give computers are ____c____ .
   (a) floppy disks   (b) sounds   (c) programs

4. People type instructions for a computer on a ____b____ .
   (a) monitor   (b) keyboard   (c) printer

5. Space on a ____a____ can get used up.
   (a) hard disk   (b) keyboard   (c) printer

6. You can buy programs on information disks called ____c____ .
   (a) modems   (b) network services   (c) compact disks

B. Answer True or False.

1. Computers are machines that can store and work with information.
   True

2. All computers need an operating system program. ____True____

3. Computers can think. ____False____

4. Most computers can be connected to a printer. ____True____

5. Network services cannot connect computers all over the country to each other. ____False____

6. CDs hold more information than floppy disks. ____True____

7. No computers have sound or speakers. ____False____

C. Draw lines to match each computer part with the job it does.

1. monitor — connects a computer to a phone line

2. modem — shows what you type on a keyboard

3. CD-ROM disk —— stores words, sound, and even pictures

Lasers

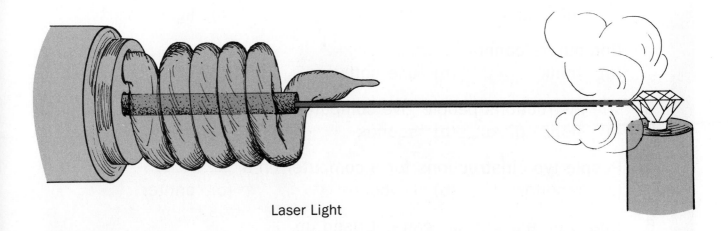

Laser Light

A **laser** is a machine that makes light travel in a narrow beam. Laser light is much stronger than natural light, which travels in all directions. Laser light is strong enough to cut diamonds and steel.

A laser beam can be small enough to drill 200 holes in the head of a pin. The spot the laser hits becomes very hot. Yet the area around it stays cool. Lasers are used in brain and eye operations. Laser light can burn away diseased body tissue without harming the healthy tissue around it. Lasers are used to remove birthmarks and tattoos. The beam itself seals up small blood vessels so there is no bleeding. Some dentists use lasers instead of drilling tools.

Lasers are also used to cut soft materials. Lasers cut the holes in baby bottle nipples. They cut the tiny holes in plastic spray bottles. They are even used to cut around patterns in some clothing factories.

Lasers can scan and record information very fast. They are used in some computer printers. They scan and record a whole page at once while other printers record letter by letter. Some laser printers can make 300 pages of sharp print in a minute. Lasers are used to scan product codes in supermarkets. Then a computer looks up the price of the item. Compact discs (CDs) are made with lasers. The signals are burned in. They never scratch or wear out.

A. Underline the correct words.

1. A laser is a machine that makes light travel in a narrow (tissue, <u>beam</u>).

2. The spot the laser hits becomes very (cold, <u>hot</u>).

3. Laser light can burn away diseased body (<u>tissue</u>, patterns) without harming the healthy tissue around it.

4. Laser light is (much weaker, <u>much stronger</u>) than natural light.

5. Laser beams can seal up small (<u>blood vessels</u>, birthmarks).

6. Lasers can be used to cut around (<u>patterns</u>, CDs) in some clothing factories.

7. Lasers can scan and record (operations, <u>information</u>) very fast.

B. Use the words below to complete the sentences.

burn	scan	travel

1. Some lasers can _____scan_____ product codes.

2. Laser light can _____burn_____ away diseased body tissue.

3. Lasers make light _____travel_____ in a narrow beam.

C. Answer True or False.

1. Lasers in computer printers can scan and record a whole page at once. ___True___

2. Instead of traveling in a narrow beam, laser light travels in all directions. ___False___

3. Some dentists use lasers instead of drilling tools. ___True___

4. Laser light cannot cut diamonds. ___False___

5. Natural light is stronger than laser light. ___False___

Robots

Robots can do many kinds of jobs.

A **robot** is a machine that can do tasks by itself. Robots can't think. Their "brains" are computers. People program the computers to do the tasks. Before computers, a machine could only do one task. Computer-controlled robots can do many different tasks. Some robots are made to look human and are programmed to do household chores.

Machine-looking robots are often used in factories. They do the hot, heavy, boring, and dangerous jobs people don't want to do. Robots paint cars because breathing paint is harmful to humans. In Tennessee, a monkeylike robot scoots along power lines to look for problems. Robots clean windows on tall buildings. We also use robots to explore deep in the ocean and outer space.

Robots are used in amusement parks and movies. They become wild animals, monsters, people with super powers, and aliens. Some robots are programmed to talk or make animal sounds.

Doctors use robots to help them with their jobs. A robot can hold a camera or a light during an operation. The robot doesn't get tired, and it can hold the light steady. Eye operations require great care and precision. Robots do well at helping doctors do eye operations.

Scientists are working on using robots to do operations in places where there are no doctors. One day this new technology will save many lives that otherwise would have been lost.

A. Answer True or False.

1. A robot is a machine that can do tasks by itself. _____True_____

2. Robots are never used in factories. _____False_____

3. A robot's "brain" is a computer. _____True_____

4. A monkeylike robot can be used to scoot along power lines to look for problems. _____True_____

5. Robots help doctors do operations. _____True_____

6. Some robots can think. _____False_____

7. Robots are used in amusement parks. _____True_____

8. Before computers, a machine could do many tasks. _____False_____

9. Robots can explore deep in the ocean. _____True_____

B. Fill in the missing words.

1. Robots are used to do jobs that are _____dangerous_____ for people. (dangerous, fun)

2. A robot doesn't get _____tired_____ during an operation and can hold a light or a camera steady. (rescued, tired)

3. Some robots are _____programmed_____ to talk or make animal sounds. (programmed, cleaned)

4. Robots paint cars because breathing paint is _____harmful_____ to humans. (harmful, healthful)

5. A _____robot_____ is a machine that can do tasks by itself. (television, robot)

C. Use each word to write a sentence about robots.

1. factories _____ Sentences will vary. _____

_____

2. computers _____

_____

Communications

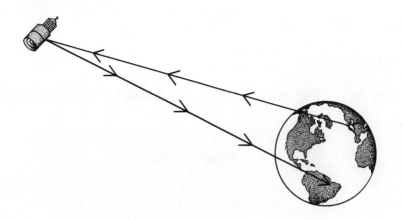

Communications Satellite

Communication is the sending and receiving of information. Whenever you talk to someone, you are communicating. Whenever you write a letter, or send a picture to a friend, you are communicating. Today, people can communicate with others all over the world.

Technology makes modern communications possible. Technology is the use of science to develop new machines. Today, people use telephones, radio, television, computers, and fax machines to communicate. Fax machines are used for sending printed information or photos over a long distance. Computers can share information with other computers in different places.

Communications satellites send signals long distances. A satellite is an object that orbits, or moves around, Earth. The moon is a natural satellite. Communications satellites are made by people and sent into space. Signals are sent from Earth to a satellite. The satellite makes the signals stronger. Then it sends them to other satellites or to a new place on Earth.

Signal towers make cellular phones work. As the phone changes location, the signals are sent to different towers. The towers make the signals stronger and pass them on.

Use the words below to complete the sentences.

communicating	photos	share
information	satellites	signals

1. Communication is the sending and receiving of ___information___ .

2. Whenever you talk to someone, you are ___communicating___ .

3. Communications ___satellites___ send signals long distances.

4. Fax machines are used for sending printed information or ___photos___ over a long distance.

5. Computers can ___share___ information with other computers in different places.

6. A satellite makes ___signals___ stronger.

B. **Answer True or False.**

1. Today people can communicate with others all over the world. ___True___

2. Computers cannot share information with other computers in different places. ___False___

3. A satellite is an object that orbits Earth. ___True___

4. A satellite makes the signals sent to it weaker. ___False___

5. As a cellular phone changes location, signals are sent to only one signal tower. ___False___

6. Signal towers make signals from cellular phones stronger and then pass on the signals. ___True___

C. **List five machines that are used for communication.** ___telephones, radio, television, computers, fax machines___

133

Technology of the Future

This fax machine and cellular phone are machines that help people communicate.

Scientists like to make machines smaller and more powerful. They also like machines to be able to do many things. How big do you think a TV, radio, telephone, fax, and tape recorder need to be? Would you believe the size of a bar of soap? The pictures from the TV would be projected on a wall by a laser beam.

What scientists want most of all is to make machines that can talk with people. Some cars can talk. They can give directions on how to find an address. Some computers can turn spoken words into printed words. But this isn't enough.

Some telephone systems can recognize voices. You can say, "Call Mom," and they will dial the right number. But this still isn't enough. The machine has to be able to understand speech. Then scientists will have successfully made artificial intelligence.

Underline the correct words.

1. If scientists can make machines that can understand speech, then they will have made (artificial intelligence, lasers).

2. Scientists like to make machines smaller and (more powerful, weaker).

3. Some (radios, computers) can turn spoken words into printed words.

134

Part A

Underline the correct words.

1. (Telephones, <u>Computers</u>) are machines that can store and work with information.

2. A (robot, <u>satellite</u>) is an object that orbits Earth.

3. Lasers can seal up small (<u>blood vessels</u>, birthmarks) so there is no bleeding.

4. (<u>Robots</u>, Laser light) can be used to do jobs that are dangerous to people.

5. Most robots have (fax machines, <u>computers</u>) inside them.

6. Whenever you talk to someone, you are (<u>communicating</u>, conducting).

7. As (keyboards, <u>cellular phones</u>) change locations, signals are sent to different towers.

Part B

Read each sentence. Write <u>True</u> if the sentence is true. Write <u>False</u> if the sentence is false.

1. The monitor is used to type instructions for a computer. _____False_____

2. Laser light is much stronger than natural light. _____True_____

3. Laser light travels in all directions. _____False_____

4. An operating system program is usually installed on a hard disk. _____True_____

5. The hand of a robot is very steady. _____True_____

6. Fax machines are used for sending music. _____False_____

7. Scientists do not want to make artificial intelligence. _____False_____

Design a Robot

You Need
- drawing paper
- lined writing paper

1. Robots can do many useful jobs. If you could design a robot, what job would you want it to do? Would it be a chore you do at home? Would it be work in your community?

2. Design a robot. Think about what features the robot would need in order to do its job. For example, if you want your robot to vacuum, it would need to sense where the furniture is.

3. Draw a picture of your robot doing its job.

4. Write a paragraph explaining how your robot does its job.

5. Explain your design to your classmates, and ask if they have any suggestions to improve your robot. If you like, revise your design based on their suggestions.

Rug Cleaning Robot

Write the Answer

It is better for robots to do some types of jobs instead of people. Give an example and explain why.

Some jobs, such as painting cars and airplanes,

involve chemicals. The chemicals may be dangerous to people,

so it is better for robots to do such tasks.

Fill in the circle in front of the word or phrase that best completes each sentence. The first one is done for you.

1. Computers are machines that can store and work with
   - ● information.
   - ⓑ electricity.
   - ⓒ superconductors.

2. Compared to natural light, laser light is
   - Ⓐ stronger.
   - ⓑ weaker.
   - ⓒ the same.

3. Today people can communicate with others
   - ⓐ only in the city.
   - ⓑ only in their state.
   - Ⓒ all over the world.

4. The spot where the laser hits becomes
   - ⓐ cold.
   - ⓑ diseased.
   - Ⓒ hot.

5. Communications satellites receive signals and
   - Ⓐ make them stronger.
   - ⓑ make them weaker.
   - ⓒ increase their frequency.

6. If machines can be made that understand speech, then we will have
   - ⓐ lasers.
   - ⓑ computers.
   - Ⓒ artificial intelligence.

Fill in the missing words.

7. A laser is a machine that makes light travel in a narrow

   _____beam_____. (tissue, beam)

8. The part of a computer that is used to type instructions for the

   computer to use is the _____keyboard_____. (keyboard, monitor)

9. A _____CD-ROM disk_____ can store words, sound, and pictures.
   (CD-ROM disk, floppy disk)

Write the answer on the lines.

10. Why are robots useful?

   Robots are useful because they are machines that can do

   many different tasks by themselves.

 acceleration, page 98.
Acceleration is a change in velocity. Speeding up is positive acceleration, and slowing down is negative acceleration.

acid, page 30.
An acid is a compound made of molecules that have a positive electric charge. Acids taste sour and turn blue litmus paper red. Strong acids can dissolve metal.

alkali, page 30.
An alkali is a base that can be dissolved in water.

alternating current, page 76.
Alternating current happens when the electron flow changes directions. The electric outlets in a house provide alternating current electricity.

amperes, page 78.
Electric current is measured in amperes. The number of amperes tells how strong the current is.

amplitude, page 54.
The amplitude of a wave is one half the distance between the wave's crest and its trough.

atom, page 8.
An atom is a tiny piece of matter. Atoms are made of three kinds of particles: protons, neutrons, and electrons.

atomic number, page 16.
The atomic number of an element is the number of protons in the nucleus of one of its atoms. No two elements have the same atomic number.

auditory canal, page 60.
The auditory canal is a tube in the ear. Sound waves move down the auditory canal to the eardrum.

auditory nerves, page 60.
The auditory nerves turn the movements of hairs inside the ear into signals. Then the nerves send the signals to the brain.

 base, page 30.
A base is a compound made of molecules that have a negative electric charge. Bases taste bitter, feel soapy, and turn red litmus paper blue.

battery, page 82.
A battery is two or more dry cells working together. A battery is used to start a car's engine.

chemical change, page 26.
A chemical change happens whenever there is a change in a substance's molecules. In a chemical change, energy causes atoms to break free of their molecules and form new, different molecules.

chemical energy, page 36.
Chemical energy is released when fuels are burned.

chemical reaction, page 28.
A chemical reaction is a chemical change. In chemical reactions, molecules are changed.

circuit, page 78.
An electric circuit is the path taken by an electric current.

circuit breaker, page 80.
A circuit breaker is a kind of switch that works like a fuse. It can break a circuit if the current is too great.

communication, page 132.
Communication is the sending and receiving of information.

compound, page 20.
A compound is a substance that is made from molecules of more than one element. A compound differs from the elements it is made of.

compound machine, page 118.
A compound machine is a simple machine connected to one or more other simple machines. In a compound machine, the force passed on to one simple machine is made larger and passed on to another.

computer, page 126.
Computers are machines that store and work with information.

concave, page 68.
A concave lens is thinner in the middle than it is at the edges. It bends light rays so that they spread apart.

conduct, page 12.
Metals conduct heat and electricity. That is, they let heat and electricity pass through them.

conduction, page 40.
The way heat passes through solids is called conduction.

conductor, page 76.
A conductor is a kind of matter that electrons can move through easily. Metal wire is a common conductor.

convection, page 40.
Convection is the way heat passes through liquids and gases.

convection current, page 40.
A convection current is the movement of molecules in a liquid or a gas when it is heated.

convex, page 68.
A convex lens is thicker in the middle than it is at the edges. It bends light rays so that they come together.

cornea, page 70.
The cornea is the thin covering of the eyeball. It helps protect the eye.

crest, page 54.
The crest is the highest part of a wave.

current electricity, page 76.
Current electricity is the movement of electrically charged particles in the same direction.

D **direct current,** page 76.
Direct current happens when the electron flow is in the same direction all the time. Batteries produce direct current electricity.

dry cell, page 82.
A dry cell is a container that holds a paste of chemicals. As the chemicals react, a flow of electrons forms a direct electric current.

ductile, page 12.
Ductile materials can be easily shaped into a new form. Metals are ductile.

E **eardrum,** page 60.
The eardrum is a thin piece of skin across the auditory canal. Sound waves make the eardrum vibrate.

electric charge, page 8.
An atom has an electric charge when the number of its electrons is not the same as the number of its protons.

electric energy, page 36.
Electric energy is energy in the form of electricity. It makes light bulbs light up and radios play.

electricity, page 74.
Electricity is caused by matter that has an electric charge.

electromagnet, page 86.
An electromagnet is formed when electricity flows through a coil of wire around an iron bar.

electromagnetic induction, page 86.
When a magnet is moved in and out of a coil of wire, electricity flows through the coil. This way of making electricity is electromagnetic induction.

electron, page 8.
An electron is a particle that moves around the nucleus of an atom. It has a negative electric charge.

electronics, page 90.
Electronics is the branch of science that makes things such as radios, stereos, televisions, calculators, and computers.

element, page 10.
An element is the simplest form of matter. It is made of only one kind of atom and cannot be broken down into different substances.

energy, page 36.
Energy is the ability to do work. There are several kinds of energy: mechanical, heat, electric, and chemical.

engine, page 120.
An engine is a compound machine. Some engines use gasoline as fuel.

eyeball, page 70.
The eyeball is the main part of the eye. It is almost round.

F **filament,** page 66.
A filament is a small piece of wire in a light bulb. When electricity passes through the wire, the wire gets hot and gives off light.

focus, page 68.
To focus means to bring light rays together at a point.

force, page 100.
A force is any push or pull. Forces may differ in size or direction.

frame of reference, page 96.
A frame of reference is some other object to which you compare an object's position.

frequency, page 54.
Frequency is the number of waves that move past one spot in a second.

friction, page 112.
Friction is the force that resists, or works against, motion. It is the rubbing of one object against another.

fulcrum, page 116.
A fulcrum is a point on which a lever can turn.

fuse, page 80.
A fuse is a device that is put in a circuit. If the circuit has too much current, the fuse wire melts and breaks the circuit.

G **gas,** page 6.
A gas is a state of matter. In a gas, the tiny particles of matter are far apart from one another.

generator, page 44.
A generator is a device that makes electricity by electromagnetic induction. Water or steam turbines are used to run generators.

gravity, pages 4, 102.
Gravity is a force that attracts, or pulls on, matter. On Earth, gravity attracts all matter to the ground.

H **heat energy,** page 36.
Heat energy is energy passed as heat from one object to another.

I **inclined plane,** page 116.
An inclined plane is a flat surface that slopes, such as a ramp.

inert gas, page 14.
An inert gas is a gas that is slow to combine with other elements. Helium is an inert gas.

insulator, page 76.
An insulator is a kind of matter that electrons cannot move through easily. Rubber is a good insulator.

ions, page 30
Ions are atoms or groups of atoms that have lost or gained one or more electrons. Because of this gain or loss, an ion has a positive or a negative electric charge.

iris, page 70.
The iris is the colored part of the eye. The iris changes the size of the pupil to let in the right amount of light.

L **larynx,** page 62.
The larynx, or voice box, is the top part of the windpipe. It holds the vocal cords that produce speech.

laser, page 128.
A laser is a machine that makes light that is much stronger than natural light. Laser light has waves of only one wavelength, all traveling in the same direction.

lenses, page 68.
Lenses are pieces of glass or other materials that can bend light.

lever, page 116.
A lever is a rod that can turn on a point, called a fulcrum. If you push down on the end of one kind of lever, the other end moves up.

liquid, page 6.
A liquid is a state of matter. In a liquid, the tiny particles of matter are farther apart than in a solid. A liquid takes the shape of its container.

M **magnet,** page 84.
A magnet is a metal that can attract and repel other pieces of metal.

magnetic field, page 84.
A magnetic field is an attracting area around a magnet.

magnetism, page 84.
Magnetism is a pulling force that certain metals have.

mass, page 4.
Mass is a measure of how much matter an object has. The mass of an object never changes.

matter, page 4.
Matter is anything that takes up space and has mass. The whole world is made of matter.

mechanical energy, page 36.
Whenever anything moves, it is using mechanical energy.

membrane, page 60
A membrane is a thin, soft, flexible layer of tissue, like the eardrum.

metal, page 12.
A metal is an element that conducts heat and electricity. Many metals are shiny and are easy to shape. Most elements are metals.

metalloid, page 14.
A metalloid is an element that is shiny like a metal but does not conduct heat and electricity well. Silicon is a metalloid.

microchip, page 90.
A microchip is a small piece of silicon that holds many transistors.

mixture, page 22.
A mixture is a combination of elements and compounds in which no new substances are formed.

molecule, page 20.
A molecule is a group of atoms. Most matter can be broken down into molecules.

motion, page 96.
Motion means moving. An object is in motion only in relation to other objects.

neutron, page 8.
A neutron is a particle in the nucleus of an atom. It has no electric charge.

nonmetal, page 14.
A nonmetal is an element that is not like a metal. Nonmetals can be solids, liquids, or gases. Carbon, oxygen, and nitrogen are nonmetals.

nuclear energy, page 48.
Nuclear energy is the energy given off when the nuclei of atoms split.

nuclear reactor, page 48.
A nuclear reactor is a place where nuclear energy is produced.

nucleus, page 8.
The nucleus is the center of an atom. Protons and neutrons are in the nucleus.

optic nerve, page 70.
The optic nerve in the eye sends messages from the retina to the brain. The brain sees the messages as pictures.

percussion instrument, page 58.
A percussion instrument makes sounds by being struck. A drum is a percussion instrument.

periodic table, page 16.
The periodic table is a scientific chart that lists all 109 elements. The elements are arranged in rows according to their atomic numbers.

photon, page 64.
A photon is a tiny particle of light that has no mass. Photons travel in waves.

physical change, page 24.
A physical change is any change in matter that does not change the matter's molecules. When matter changes states, a physical change takes place.

pitch, page 56.
The pitch of a sound is the quality of being high or low. A sound's pitch is based on the frequency of its sound waves.

plasma, page 6.
Plasma is a state of matter that is not common on Earth. The sun, most of the stars, and lightning are plasma.

pole, page 84.
A pole is the end of a magnet. All magnets have a north pole and a south pole.

prism, page 67.
A prism is a piece of glass shaped like a triangle. A prism separates light into its different colors.

program, page 126.
A program is a set of instructions for a computer.

proton, page 8.
A proton is a particle in the nucleus of an atom. It has a positive electric charge.

pulley, page 116.
A pulley is a wheel with a rope around it. Pulleys can be used to lift objects.

pupil, page 70.
The pupil is a hole in the middle of the eye. Light enters the eye through the pupil. The size of the pupil is changed by the iris to let in the right amount of light.

radiation, page 40.
Radiation is one way of passing heat energy. Radiation moves in waves. Heat comes from the sun in radiation waves.

rays, page 64.
Light travels in straight lines called rays.

reflection, page 64.
Reflection takes place when light rays hit a smooth surface and bounce back.

refraction, page 64.
Refraction takes place when light rays are bent by things in their path.

retina, page 70.
> The retina is the lining at the back of the eye. It is attached to the optic nerve.

robot, page 130.
> A robot is a machine that can do tasks by itself. Most robots have computers inside them.

rotate, page 66.
> To rotate means to spin around. Earth rotates.

salt, page 30.
> A salt is a compound that is formed when an acid and an alkali neutralize each other.

satellite, pages 106, 132.
> A satellite is an object that orbits, or moves around, Earth. The moon is a natural satellite.

screw, page 116.
> A screw is an inclined plane wrapped around a rod. Screws hold things together well.

semiconductor, page 90.
> A semiconductor is a kind of matter that is not a very good conductor or insulator. It can control an electric current in an electronic device.

short circuit, page 78.
> In a short circuit, electrical wires that should be separate touch each other. Then electrons can move from wire to wire, taking a shortcut through the circuit. A short circuit can start a fire.

silicon, page 90.
> Silicon is an element that is used as a semiconductor.

simple machine, page 116.
> A simple machine is a device that makes work easier. All machines are based on the six simple machines: the lever, inclined plane, wedge, screw, pulley, and wheel and axle.

software, page 126.
> Software is a set of programs for a computer.

solar energy, page 38.
> Solar energy is energy from the sun. On Earth, solar energy is changed to other kinds of energy.

solid, page 6.
> A solid is a state of matter. In a solid, the tiny particles of matter are held very closely together. A solid holds its shape.

solution, page 22.
> A solution is a mixture in which one substance is dissolved in another. Most solutions are liquids, but some are solids.

spectrum, page 67.
> The spectrum is all the colors of light. The spectrum can be seen through the use of a prism.

speed, page 98.
> Speed is the distance something moves in a certain time.

state, page 6.
> A state is a form of matter. Matter can exist in four states: solid, liquid, gas, and plasma.

static electricity, page 74.
> The attraction we can see between two objects with opposite electric charges is called static electricity.

steam, page 46.
> When water boils, it turns into a gas called steam. Steam can push on objects and move them.

steam turbine, page 46.
> A steam turbine is a kind of wheel with blades. Steam turbines can turn a ship's propellers. They can also be used to make electricity.

stringed instrument, page 58.
> A stringed instrument makes sounds by vibrating strings. A guitar is a stringed instrument.

technology, page 132.
> Technology is the use of science to develop new machines.

terminal, page 82.
> A terminal is a post of a dry cell. One terminal is negative, and the other is positive. When a wire is put between the two terminals, a circuit is made.

transistor, page 90.
> A transistor is a tiny device used to change current electricity into signals.

trough, page 54.
> The trough is the lowest part of a wave.

velocity, page 98.
Velocity is speed in a certain direction.

vocal cords, page 62.
The vocal cords are small bands of tissue on either side of the voice box, or larynx. Vibrations of the vocal cords are the sounds that make up speech.

volts, page 78.
The amount of push a source of electricity gives the electricity is measured in volts. The number of volts tells how easily the current can move through a circuit.

water turbine, page 44.
A water turbine is a device that turns water energy into mechanical energy. This energy can be used to run a generator that makes electricity.

wavelength, page 54.
Wavelength is the distance between the crests of two waves.

wedge, page 116.
A wedge is two inclined planes that come together in a point.

wheel and axle, page 116.
A wheel and axle is a kind of lever that continues to turn around its fulcrum.

wind instrument, page 58.
A wind instrument makes sounds by a vibrating column of air inside the instrument. A saxophone is a wind instrument.

windpipe, page 62.
The windpipe is a tube in the throat. Air moving up through the windpipe makes the vocal cords vibrate. Then sounds are made.

work, page 110.
Work is the use of force to move an object.

Acknowledgments

Illustrations

Alex Bloch—**98, 100, 102, 104, 110, 112, U4A, 116, 117, 118, 120**

Leslie Dunlap—**18, 34, 52. 72, 94**

David Griffin—**6A, 6D, 76, 114B**

Kathie Kelleher—**108, 124, 136**

Erika Kors—**4, 8, 12, 20, 22, 24, 28, 30, 32, 40, 56, 58, 60, 62, 82, 84, 96, 97, 128, 132**

Tek-Nek, Inc.—**6B, 6C, 16, 54**

Stephen Turner—**66**

All Other Illustrations

Ben Smith and Jessie Flores

Photographs

P.**10 (top)** Christina Dittmann/Rainbow, **(middle)** Carl Purcell/Words and Pictures, **(bottom)** Dan McCox/Rainbow; p.**14 (right)** T.J. Florian/Rainbow; p.**20** Tennessee State Library and Archives; p.**26 (left)** © Dennis MacDonald/PhotoEdit, **(right)** © Viki Miller/In Stock; p.**36 (left)** © Aneal Vohra/Unicorn Stock Photos, **(right)** © Tony Freeman/PhotoEdit; p.**44** US Department of the Interior; p.**48** © Grant Heilman Photography; p.**50 (left)** © Grant Heilman Photography, **(right)** © David Doody/Tom Stack & Associates; p.**54** © Tony Freeman/PhotoEdit; p.**64** © Jeff Greenberg; p.**74** National Weather Service; p.**86** Caterpillar, Inc.; p.**88** Courtesy Press of Ohio; p.**90** © James A. Sugar/CORBIS; p.**92** Victoria Beller Smith; p.**106** National Oceanic and Atmospheric Association.

Additional photography by Royalty-Free/CORBIS, Comstock Royalty Free, Digital Vision/Getty Royalty Free, PhotoDisc/Getty Royalty Free, and Photos.com Royalty Free.